GROWING PAINS

Edited By

TRUDI PURDY

First published in Great Britain in 1993 by
ARRIVAL PRESS
3 Wulfric Square, Bretton,
Peterborough, PE3 8RF

FOREWORD

Everyone comes across a problem or two whilst trying to make it through their teens in one piece! I decided to try and put this book together as a sort of handbook for teenagers and it is certainly that! Although it doesn't give answers to all adolescent hiccups, *Growing Pains* lets Teenagers know that they are not the only ones to have to go through this real *pain-in-the-butt* time. It lets them know that they are not alone!

The problems that pop up between the ages of 10 and 17 are expressed here for all to see. I know whilst reading this book you will definitely be able to identify with each and every poem. Take hope in the fact that others have been through this and more will have it to come! Enjoy!

Trudi Purdy

Contents

In my Day

I was born in seventy eight -
To two good folks as was my Fate,
They seem so old and out of date,
Know only one phrase - *in my day.*

This applies and compares to all I do,
I do some weird things, yet it's true,
All must be criticized and challenged too -
And of course compared to *in my day.*

I'd like to go back to this *day* of theirs
To see why my reactions get stony glares,
I don't expect to creep up the stairs
If late - as they did in *my day.*

My skirts are short, my dress is loud,
Is it a crime to stand out in a crowd?
To show off what Nature has generously endowed,
P'raps not now - but yes, *in my day.*

Now I've reached twelve to nineteen between
Can they survive the rest of my teens?
When I'm too old to wear my jeans
Will I be quoting *in my day?*

Margaret Barrett

I Want to be Me!

I've done it now, it's past my deadline,
Late and I know what I'll hear,
Grounded for a week and help in the house,
I'm not a child, I'm seventeen,
But they've forgotten, young!
Were they ever young? Do they really care!
Shouting and ordering, that's all I hear.
Don't they know I'm almost an adult!
I can think for myself, I have opinions,
I want to talk, I want to be heard.
It's for your own good they say,
10.30 is late enough in the day.
I want to be out with my friends,
I want to let the world know, I'm Here!

Hilary Chaplin

Modern Teenager

Looks that others envy,
A nature of sugar and spice,
Happy, lucky girl.

So like her Father,
Opposite to her Mother,
Clashes with sister.

Grows at own speed,
Worries her parents silly,
To their distraction.

Quick mighty temper,
Storm and calm alternate,
Dreams of schemes.

Trailing laces follow
Jacket worn open, flapping,
Proudly uses dirty trainers.

Clothes heaps sulk discarded,
Dates evoke frantic dances,
Bedroom without care.

Spare her the rod?
Withdraw all her privileges?
Face the angry noise?

Easy to disagree with,
Impossible to dislike,
Cannot live without.

Andrew Trybalski

That's Life

'Why are you square in this house?'
Is queried umpteen times a day.
When *teens* think their parents are fogies
Why don't they move away?

I'm sick of the sound of computers,
The bleep of electronic games,
I find fearfully wearing the rock music blaring
Of pop groups with very weird names.

Not a bed's been made, not a curtain drawn,
There are clothes all over the floor.
We're subjected to teenage tempers,
The frequent slamming of doors,
And sotto voce mutterings of
'Square parents are such bores.'

I was a teenager too, you know,
Oh yes, I remember it well.
I thought my parents square, they drove me spare:
I probably gave them hell.

Remember, my dears, when your turn comes
And you are parents too,
Teens drive you mad, but they aren't all bad:
They're entitled to their point of view.

When you have upped and offed shall I
Suffer *empty nest* syndrome?
Rue the day you moved away
And wish you were all back home?

I wonder - why did we have them?
We were younger and greener then.
But, given the choice, we'd reply with one voice
'We'd go through it all again!'

Elspeth Wallington

The Happiest Days of Your Life

Who bullies the bully
And tells them what to do?
I ache inside, to fight your fight
But I know it has to be you.
You've always been so gentle
Knew you had to share
We should have taught survival
For the jungle that's out there.

Gone my happy laughing child
To nights of endless crying.
The transition from story-book world
Is hard
Your innocence is dying.

Perhaps one day you'll fit in
Be just the same as the rest.
Until you do
I think you'll find
Solitare's the game that's best.

Wendy Henley

What do Parents Know

What do parents know
Of teenage highs and lows
Of heartache dull that springs
From unrequited love's heartstrings
What do they know
Of boredoms grind
Of money short
And fashions bind
Too young to understand
Too old to be *in the band*
It's hard to be a teeny
Pity parents are such meanies
You wouldn't think that *they*
Were teenagers themselves one day.

Roy Whitfield

The First Kiss

I'd waited all evening, to sample her lips,
I'd walked her home, I'd even bought her some chips,
We held hands up to reaching her gate,
Her Mother was waiting, 'H'm, you two are late.'
I thought you'd be here by a quarter past ten,
I've walked to the gate here, again and again.'
We came straight home I told her, after the dance,
We didn't have time for a little romance,
All right then I'll leave you to say goodnight,
She walked in the house then, and switched off the light,
My arms round my sweetheart we cuddled up close,
Head on my shoulder, her hair tickled my nose,
I bent down to sample, those luscious red lips,
But all that I got was the taste of her chips.

Edna Watford Harvey

Twelve

You are twelve, grown tall,
Not yet a man.
Already you know about cars
And motorbikes
And wish you were eighteen.

You are twelve, into videos
And computer games.
You have a bike that's always breaking
And needs new tyres
And girls are not your scene.

You are twelve, grown up you say,
'I'll get a job,
I need money for the weekend,
If it doesn't rain
I'm going out all day.'

You are twelve, you got detention
For being late
And homework is such a nuisance.
Friends are waiting
For you to go and play.

You are twelve, doing fine,
Always eating,
Or fidgeting or arguing.
Never mind
Be patient if you can.

You are twelve, long legs
With clumsy feet
But some day soon you won't be twelve,
You'll be eighteen,
You'll be a man.

Patricia Catling

Absent Love

Oh heart don't weep
But sleep
And in the morning
She will be here. . .
. . . (please, please. . .)

Alfred Dewsbury

Fashion Freak

My teenage years were filled with doubt,
At what was In and what was Out,
Should hair be long, or short and neat,
What shoes to wear upon my feet?

How to keep up with the trend,
Scoring points with my best friend,
Search high and low for stylish gear,
Without streetcred my greatest fear.

Now, trainers hold the greatest sway,
And leggings are the *look* today,
Such brightly coloured fashion flair,
Oh, how I wish now that I could dare!

Glenda Lawrence

First Kiss

My mind is in turmoil,
My emotions on trial;
I'm enveloped in your presence,
Overcome by your smile.
I've never felt this way,
About anyone but you;
Your hair, oakwood brown,
Your eyes, midnight blue.
My heart is a fountain;
The next beat it will miss;
As your lips touch mine. . .
For my very first kiss.

Gianna Pollero (14)

The Room

We painted the room in pink and white.
Delicate nets and flower sprigged fabric.
Feminine touches, frilly and bright.
Perfect, pleasant, romantic.

She plastered the walls, ceiling to floor.
Picture, pin-up and poster.
Save the Whale and Feed the Poor.
Liberate, emulate, foster.

Order and harmony fled from the place.
Confusion and chaos reign.
Clothes tossed in heaps, fill every space.
Decorate, obstruct, remain.

Deafening music that plummets and soars. . .
Mandatory, early and late.
Erupting forth from windows and doors.
Disordant, permanent state.

Door shut fast on a gather of girls
Face pack, make-up and cream.
Gilding fair faces, creating curls.
Whisper, giggle and dream.

Diane Watson

Day Trip
(For Wosername at Felixstowe)

Kiss me Kiss me,
Kiss Me Quick
You wore it on your hat,
kiss me kiss me,
Kiss Me Quick
I stopped,
and did just that.
Seaside romance
on pebbled beach
mid hotdogs greasy smell,
you blue jeaned and apple cheeked
I kissed your lips and fell.
Walking arm in arm, and free
on promenade and pier,
oh happy seaside, happy us
would it could last all year.

I walked you to the Bus Station
then, one final kiss,
promised letters never sent
we both said we would miss.

Seaside romance,
Kiss And Quick
that's all right with me,
kiss and run
seaside trip,
and home in time for tea.

J N Cates

The Two Teenagers

As I was riding on a bus,
I heard two teenagers making a fuss,
The one unto the other did say,
I'm running away from home today.

Then said the other to her mate,
Oh why are you in such a state?
What's causing you to feel this way?
That you want to run away.

It's that house of mine it's so frustrating,
My brother he's always agitating,
My Dad he never stops complaining,
My Mother too, they're always saying.

That my room's always in a mess,
That I look really weird the way I dress,
And that I pick some awful queer friends,
In my house it just never ends.

And if things go missing it's always the same,
Because when someone has to take the blame,
Then you can guarantee it's always me,
No it's never them, how could it be!

Yes I know what you mean then said her mate,
With all that you're saying I can relate,
In fact the more you talk about your home,
The more it sounds just like my own.

So she said, if you're running away today,
Then please don't let me stop you,
In fact wait a minute, don't leave me behind,
Because I'm coming too.
Kevin Fitzgerald

No Longer a Child

No longer a child, but not yet an adult,
This teenage era has given me a jolt,
Too young for this, too old for that,
I'll work it out as here I'm sat.

The music is too loud, I must not be late,
There is an inquisition if I have a date,
Tidy your bedroom, stop moping around,
These comments, have become a familiar sound.

I'm bored, fed up, I've got nothing to do,
I've nothing to wear and need something new,
Nobody understands me around this place,
Sometimes I feel like packing my case.

I ask myself where would I go,
After much deliberation I tell myself no,
Three meals a day, a nice warm pad,
I'll stay here and annoy me Mum and Dad.

No wait, that's not fair, it is not right,
It's me who continually wants to fight,
It's me hormones, they say, they are all upset,
But never mind, baby, do not fret.

I want to be an adult, not an in-between,
Because being a teenager is real, real mean,
It's me emotional state playing tricks on me,
I'll be glad when a teenager, I'll no longer be.

Jacqui Weeks

Growing Pains and Daffodil Tea

I never had those teenage spots, nor acne on my face,
Never lacked self-confidence, never felt out of place.
Growing Pains? I had a few, but strictly between me and you . . .
A hiccough, every now and then, upset my equilibrium,
Throwing me off balance and into near delirium.

I once was asked to sing a song, for the Old Folks, you see,
The auspicious occasion was the Church Daffodil Tea -
I stumbled up the wooden steps - fell flat upon the stage,
To add insult to injury, the pianist lost the page!
I didn't know whether to laugh, or just sit down and cry,
I wished the floor would open up - I just wanted to die!

The Old Folks were watching me, there was a pregnant pause,
But as I started singing, to the sound of their applause,
A warm glow stole over me - there wasn't a dry eye,
As I sang, unaccompanied, my Scottish Lullaby.
Growing Pains? I had a few, but strictly between me and you . . .

I remember my first kiss, my Prince Charming, oh, what bliss,
He told me I was beautiful and swore undying love,
Until Miss Gorgeous came along and push turned into shove!
I tried so hard to bear in mind, the old adage that *Love is Blind!*
My *Growing Pains* were very few, and strictly between me and you,
I somehow managed to pull through . . . *what else can a body do?*

Nancy Gray

Life

Boring . . . boring,
I'm bored.
Bored to tears,
bored to death,
- *Dead* boring!

Boring . . . snoring.
Too tired to bother,
too bored to care
- movement rare.

Minutes, hours, days,
time to spare.
Freedom hangs heavy,
turning to despair.

No inspiration,
imagination dim.
Brain just ticking over
- prospects grim!

Jennifer Allen

Thirteen Yesterday

My hair is lank, I have a face full of pimples
Whatever happened to my blonde hair and dimples
I know I've suddenly grown a bit bigger
And developed what is called a figure

They say that I've reached puberty
But that doesn't mean very much to me
It was my thirteenth birthday yesterday
But I don't feel different in any way

They say I'm a woman now, not a girl
I'm afraid my head is in a whirl
I still don't feel grown-up you see
Whatever I am supposed to be

I don't want to think about make-up and boys
I'm happy for now just to play with my toys!

Jennifer Ann Reid

The Perfectionist

I practised on my mirror the other day,
To see if I could kiss in the right sort of way,
It made me confident, it made me feel fine,
For tonight I will kiss for real this time.

We sat at the back of the movie show,
So I said to myself 'Ah well here we go,'
I put my hand around her back,
I tilted my head to give her a smack,
Her lips were warm and tasted of gum,
Then she spoiled it all when she stuck out her tongue.

E Larkin

Heart Flutters at Ye Old Antique Shoppe

The dark girl ignores her Mother's summons,
Her heart is called another way,
Her grey eyes search the summer street,
'Lunch, Molly,' the Mother calls again,
'Just a minute, I'm dusting Ted and Elsie.'
The girl picks up the figurine, kisses it.

Lovingly, her gaze strays from the vase
Up the seaside street again - then she holds
It in the sunlight above her head,
And stretches to kiss the dancing pair again;
'Delightful,' he had said, caressing them.

'Molly,' her Mother's voice is sharp,
One more furtive glance, she sees him -
And is transfixed and clasps the vase to her bosom;
Nearer, nearer, manly strides vibrate the street,
Slow down, stop, her dancing heart stops, too,
Unsteady hands place the vase on the counter.

A delicate cough. But no, not a glance -
But wait, he stands at Fen's gate - a blonde appears
And welcomes the tall giant into her house:

Dark curls wail into the duster: 'The brazen - '
Ivory hands bang the counter,
Mystified, her mother stands with her dinner
And sees the dancing pair take a suicide leap -
Molly kicks the smithereens and grabs the tray.

Mary Frances Mooney

Making the Best of Life

I'm fifteen and have a baby
A beautiful girl it is true
I live in a large youth hostel
My parents said we're through

Her Father doesn't want to know us
And most of the time I feel blue
I sit in my one room bedsit
Thinking why can't I be more like you

You are my older sister
The apple of Mum and Dad's eye
You did things the right way
They even thought you could fly

I've had enough of being second
I've decided I want to be first
I could be a landscape gardener
A vet, or even a nurse

I'm seventeen now and at college
My girl has a nursery place
I have my own flat, a friend and a cat
And a smile upon my face

I think of the times gone by
And things that I've had to face
There's nothing you can't get over
With a smile and a little good grace.

M P Newman

Susan

Coursed me pain.
I wooed her till six.
That night she gave me,
My first kiss.

I got home late.
For tea,
No tea!
Legs slapped.
Sent to bed.
Could not go out the next day.

A full day two nights I stayed in love, till,
I found out she could not play marbles.
And I did not want to skip.

Brian Walker

Hard Life

Life's hard for us teenagers
The problems that we've got,
Yesterday I had a face
Today I've got a spot.

A great enormous red thing
That obliviates my chin,
When I knock on someone's door
It's the spot that they let in.

They've stopped addressing me by name
I'm just called the *Zit*,
When it's gone my chin will have
A great enormous pit.

Then of course there are the teeth
If they don't grow straight
A wire is put into your mouth
Just like a five-bar gate.

Just fine while your mouth is closed
Full of metal filler,
But when you give a nice big smile
A certain passion killer.

Bodies are a problem
As parts begin to grow,
Not all at the same rate
Some fast, others slow.

First love, first kiss and parents
Exams and puberty,
Puppy fat and illness
How much tougher can life be?
Shelley Thomas

Youth Service

All I wanted was a fiver
to gamble on a horse,
it was a certain winner
but Mum said *'No.'* of course.
So I took a chance and grabbed a bag
from a oldie passing by,
but she hung on and yelled and that
and thumped me in the eye.
The horse came first, I knew it would,
the rest were out of sight.
The Magistrate said 'Youth Service,'
and Mum said 'Serves you right.'
After all this pain and hassle
I'm giving up on crime,
a bus-pass, key and sixty pence,
are not worth doing time.

Catherine Cheffins

I Remember

Here's to you and the games we played.
I remember still as though yesterday.
Running wild, careless, free,
away from school and glad to be.
Football days, street corner nights,
chippy suppers on benches by the traffic lights.

I remember too the plans we made,
of wealth and fame, they quickly fade.
I was going to play for England, you were going to be a rock star.
I was going to buy a Rolls Royce, you a red sports car.
Dirty jokes and more to tell,
hard face looks, yet scared as hell.
Denim jeans and motorbikes,
we posed a bit to the girls we liked.
Party nights, drinking beer,
throwing up and feeling queer.

I remember the friendship we had together,
a special bond that lasts forever.
What happened to the people we used to be?
I was going to change the world, and yet the world changed me.
We were just young lads with *nowt* to do,
growing up but not wanting to.

I remember the good times, every one,
and though they seem as clear as day,
they are long since dead and gone.

Anthony Greenwood

A Teenage Problem

I cannot see a greenhouse above me in the sky,
The cause of world-wide panic and me to reason why,
I've got to think pollution and everything it means,
Each time I use soap powder to wash my brand new jeans.

Each time I take my wheels and girlfriend for a spin,
Or with my empty coke tins fill up the rubbish bin,
I must think what I'm doing to all the air around,
And what will be the future for my coke tins in the ground.

I really must endeavour to think of it much more,
And openly acknowledge what's floating on the shore,
To urge the men in power who only have the means,
To bring about new methods for me to wash my jeans.

Perhaps they'll use a laser or ultra sonic sound,
A miracle technology I'm sure will soon be found,
To cut out using water or other natural thing,
Like gas or sun made power or windmill vanes that swing.

So please will you now tell me how I may questions solve,
About my own close problem which I can then resolve,
You see I'm keen on fashion and must, by any means,
Reduce the brand new colour from my new pair of jeans.

W Beynon

Grip of Love

Our grip of love broke
Gently we parted
I tried to forget
The dream we had started
His whispers, promises
Kisses and fears
But all that remains
Are my painful tears
His silver necklace
Is overworn
His lovely letters
Are tattered and torn.
I often wander to
The same lovers place
And dream on end
Into empty space
My thoughts were once
Of love and care
But now they too
Are deserted and bare

If only I'd known
When we met that day
That sometime when *fed-up*
You'd cast me away
If only I'd been that
Little more alert
Then perhaps our breakup
Wouldn't have hurt.

Hev Woodhouse

Resilience

Don't be downhearted
When things go so wrong
Be of good spirit
Be cheerful, be strong
Whatever your troubles
Whatever your plight
Come out of the shadows
Walk into the light
Shrug off your worries
Show a brave face
Take what's in store
With courage and grace
Bad times will come to an end
So they say
The burden will lighten
For you day by day.

Albert Beecroft

On Being a Teenager

I hate being a teenager
With hormones, spots and lank hair
Having to shower together at school
And walking around bare

With exams and sex education
Giggles and knowing stares
Parents ranting and raving
Spending all day upstairs

When will I be older
With children of my own
When will I have teenagers
So it's my turn to moan.

Margaret Smythers

Summer Love

Remember last September
Remember when we met
I never heard your name
My love
How quickly we forget

Seagulls screech
Into the cavern
The cavern on the strand
We walk along the sand
We walk
We talk
We stand
We find a spot along the beach
By a toilet wall
Hide from people walking by
We nearly did it all.

Julian Parratt

Romance in Reality

Oh how I remember when I first kissed,
I was so blind drunk, I nearly missed.
Let's think, I was twelve years old,
It was a Summer's night, but very cold.
There had been a party and he had walked me home,
At that time I wished I had been alone.
I remember his acne rubbing on my skin,
He smelt of B.O. and his clothes smelt of gin.
He name suited him, Larry. No, it was Nick.
Whatever it was, my first kiss was sick.

Paula West (17)

We are All Equal

'Nobody understands me,'
said the adolescent to his Mum,
'I'm growing up too fast for them
to stay in line.' 'My son
you must keep ahead for all your life.
Friends will come and go.
Age thirteen to age eighteen will be
hard.' 'Yes I know
but I find their humour immature,
their opinions hastily made.
I feel too old for their parties.
My teenage years are paid.

Nobody understands me, Mum,'
he said, with feelings shown,
'I have to come away from life.
I have to be alone
in the world I thought that I could change,
a world of war and pain
in places but in others we know that
some leaders are sane
enough to hold their countries
together through with truth.'
'Darling listen, you're no different,
nobody understands me too.'

Daniel Hawthorne

Mums Don't Understand

When Mum shouted at me
'cos my room was such a mess,
I told her there
just aren't enough hours
in the day
to do everything.

Mum said that was rubbish,
'cos I'd found time
to put a spider in the bath,
and kick a football
through the bedroom window.

'Some things are important,' I said.

Doreen Dean

Normal

I could pick a daisy
And wear it in my hair,
Stand upon a roof-top
And declare I do not care,

I could scream in public,
And drop a cut-glass vase,
Go and join the Navy,
Or run in front of cars,

I could leap off bridges,
With yellow wellies on my feet,
Paint my face bright purple,
And dance across the street,

I could wear weird tank-tops,
And dye my hair green,
Have a flashing beacon on my head
So surely I'd be seen. . .

But you just stand there,
And never notice me.
So I'll just walk past you
And be as normal as can be.

Melanie Watling

Teenaging

When I was a Teenager
Everything changed.
My hair went greasy
And my chest rearranged.
School became pressurised
Mum nagged at home.
I developed a craving
For using the 'phone.
I think I went deaf
Wanting everything loud
The spot on my chin
Stood out in the crowd.
I went to mad parties
And drank cheap cider.
Sat next to that Neil
With hands like a spider.
We weren't ozone friendly
We just didn't care
Our only concern
Was who was a pair.
We sprayed our deodorants
And used CFC's
Wrote pathetic notes
With no thought for the trees.
Lots of blue denim
A coat made of coney
Would I go back?
Ah - if only!

Alison Deare

Tonight's the Night

Tonight's the night - *the* night.
It'll be beautiful (not to be missed),
For tonight's the night that I receive
My very first, *very first* kiss!

The stars will shine out brighter
Than they ever have done before!
(I stop to practice my lip movements
In the mirror in the hall).

I creep outside and into the cold,
I'm a beauty, a goddess to adore!
I meet him down by the oak tree,
(We've met there once before).

He (finally) leans towards me -
I pucker my lips to meet him,
He hesitates, then continues,
And we begin our very first kiss!

It only lasted a second!
It's not how they said in the books!
I wipe my mouth across my sleeve,
And cut him some evil looks.

I trundle off homewards, disappointed.
I didn't rate it much at all!
In fact, I'd have gained more pleasure
Hitting my head against a brick wall!

Tonight was supposed to be *the* night,
(A night I now wish I'd missed),
I hope, now, that never again
Will I ever, *ever* be kissed!

Deborah Ward

Long Ago I Was Fifteen

Wearing tights, instead of socks
And an earring in one ear.
Make-up and short skirts,
Like the girls wear in fifth year.
Oh, I wish I was sixteen.

Too old for the playground,
Too young for the dance.
I'd run away and be a model,
If I had half a chance.
Oh, I wish I was sixteen.

My Mum and Dad don't really care.
It's absolutely true.
They won't let me cut my hair,
Or wear anything see-through.
Oh, I wish I was sixteen.

My Dad hates the Rolling Stones,
Says their records are a *row*
But he's as old as Moses,
So what does he know now.
Oh, I wish I was sixteen.

World War Two was raging
When my mum was sixteen,
So loads of girls wore socks
And it didn't consequently mean
That *they* weren't sixteen.

One day, I'll be sixteen
And then I'll show the world.
Pop singer, Hollywood queen
Or even a rocker's girl,
I'm going to do it all.
Oh, I wish I was sixteen.

Jennifer Bradley

A Guilty Secret

Why did I pack my bags and leave?
I ran away from life;
I felt I could not carry on
Through bitterness and strife.
I felt so lonely as each day grew,
My strength just faded away;
If I could turn the clock back now,
I would never have gone that day.
If I could have another chance
The guilt may disappear;
And maybe like the times before
My Mam and I will be near.
There won't be any fighting
Guilty sobs, and angry cries,
But maybe I'll be loved again
Instead of seeing hatred in her eyes.
I've tried so hard to say I'm sorry;
I wish I hadn't run away,
But there was so much pain and so much hurt;
I really couldn't stay.
I love you Mam
Forgive me please,
But I really had to go,
But if you could be my age again,
You'd understand, I know.

Caroline Brown

Mirror, Mirror on the Wall

He'd been in the bathroom hours and hours, door shut, barricaded, bolted
tight.
Sister's got a heavy date shouts impatiently 'Will you be in there all flippin'
night?'
The sullen face emerges, silent eyes plea, pointed finger shows the biggest
zit for us to see!
We hold our breath not daring to comment, speak or even smile
Whilst big sister laughs holding her sides as tears of laughter flow to flood
the *Nile*.
Now he's locked away in darkened room refusing solace, food or drink
Dad shakes his head in utter dismay 'Were we like this, let's think?'
We'd survived all his phases, rocker, then mod, punk bondage legs bound
his trousers, so tightly
This didn't last long for he kept missing his bus unable to run - nightly!
He'd formed a band, a group, the name was like them *The Chronic*
They made a tape, a demo job, they were bound for the charts, speed,
supersonic!
Then came the motorbike my heart sank as he lovingly polished his
Kwaka
It came with a long legged blonde astride it, Dad rubbed his hands, 'She's a
cracker,'
They all disappeared spots, band and bike for now it was girls instead,
The house smelled of after-shave, hairspray and gel and a hand-knitted
Willie Warmer adorned his bed head!
The phone never ceased ringing as he casually broke one heart after
another
Our once spotty, gangly pseudo rockstar had become the ardent lover.
Hard to imagine how this metamorphosis took place he was such a total
disaster
Now Dad looks adoringly in the mirror and smiles
'I know who he takes after!'

Joyce Hefti-Whitney

Teenage Traumas

It's not easy being a teenager, with braces, spots and glasses,
Micky taking all the time, teasing in school classes,
Boys are unknown qualities, enigmas every one,
Teenage years are full of fears, I'll be happy when they're gone!

Nights are filled with forbidden fun, discos and nightclubs,
Trying to look over eighteen and sneaking down the pub,
Experimenting with Mom's make-up, lips of brightest red,
I don't want to go to school today, I think I'll stay in bed.

I hope I have a boyfriend soon, my best friend's one is great,
She gets lots more money, and she stays up late.
Problems? Let me tell you, I know that I've got plenty,
Hurry teenage years and go, I can't wait until I'm twenty.

Sarah Cheetham

Growing Pains
(A parent's viewpoint)

I tended my prize bloom in the garden
With an abundance of loving care.
I watched her blossom as the seasons passed by
Until the day she was no longer there.

I searched in vain for her presence,
As the seasons came and went.
Then a hybrid appeared the following year
And I knew my time had been well spent.

Hannah Kellie

Night Out

Mingled between the food and drink,
Lies fatigue and boredom,
Financial guilt and thoughts of -
Meeting the Bank Manager. . .

Worries about finding a job. . .
Mingle together with social chit chat
And celebrations.

The problems in life mix
Like my gin and tonic, with -
Discussions about yesterday's weather
And the price of bread.

Alcoholic melancholia quickly turns the
Night out, into -
A surreal nightmare.

Thomas J St Clement

Soliloquy of a Teenager

They tell me I'm aggressive and maybe that is true,
But it's because I'm frightened and don't know what to do.
I tell them they're not *with it* and haven't got a clue
And that they're too dogmatic - say, maybe they're scared too!

There's such a lot of things to fear, for them as well as us.
We're scared we'll miss the jet plane, they're scared they've missed the bus!
They're frightened of me growing up, don't want to let me go.
I'm frightened too but callow pride will never let it show.

I wonder why they are so scared and if it could be so -
That in the past they also found it difficult to grow.
They wouldn't have felt so different from how I feel today -
What if they had lost their heads and really gone astray?

Supposing they're still not too old to feel that certain urge,
To break down all the barriers and suddenly emerge -
Into a world that's full of things which they don't understand?
I don't think they could cope with it, this world of shifting sand.

I'll have to watch them carefully and try to make them see,
That if they stay together it is best for them - and me!
I really couldn't bear it if they changed their steady ways.
I need them just the way they are - their sympathy and praise.

I'll really have to watch my step and set a good example.
There are too many things out there that they might like to sample!
I wonder just how strong they are to combat such temptation.
Perhaps, like me, they also feel a sense of deep frustration?

We'll have to work together to keep each other strong.
We'll have to live in harmony and learn to get along.
They have their fears and I have mine, it seems to me that's so.
Together we must walk through life and help each other grow.
Shirley H Ford

Oh Woe is Me

Oh woe is me, a spot is born upon my aquiline nose
'Don't squeeze it,' I am made aware
As pus from out it flows . . .
I try to hide it with some cream, even apply toothpaste
But on reflection I can see
It all is such a waste . . .
Perhaps a hair style will disguise, with pop star's longer quiff?
But I look just like my dog
Who has to see to sniff . . .
I can't go on like this I thought as I dreamed of my date
Perhaps a face mask will suffice
Oh woe is me, what fate . . .
I phoned my best mate straightaway 'I'll come right round,' he said
But as he came in through the door
It bled and bled and bled . . .
'Cor blimey,' he did acquiesce 'You're really in decline,'
'Get fixed up with fancy dress,'
'As Cyrano you'll be fine . . . '
I pushed him back out of the door, I wished that I could die
Mum came in with her advice
'Wear a red spotted tie . . . '
I was left in deep dismay as I listened to TV
'Red nose day,' I heard it said
So I bought one and you see
I wore it all that evening, my date thought I was fun
Now I squeeze her spots instead
And they're second to none. . .

Margarette L Damsell

The Youth Club

Well here I am
My first night in
But who's that shouting
I don't like him

With hands in pockets
And a look of glaze
I stand in a corner
And look on amazed

Do I look
Or should I talk
Should I be here
I've got second thoughts

What do I do
What do I say
If they look at me
Do I look away

I know
I'll read a poster
There's one quite near
If I read it long enough
They'll forget I'm here

O God what's the time
I want to go home
I don't like it here
I hate being alone

But what if I liked it
I'll never know
It might have been different
It they'd said hallo

Jim Kerr

Alligators and Elves

When you were an innocent twelve,
Did you start to disbelieve in the Elves?
Awakening thirteen,
Did you scrutinize the mirror and wonder:
'Is my face and teeth clean?'
One year later,
Did you feel and look like an ugly alligator?
Such are the long teenage days,
Full of self-doubt, unanswered questions;
A vast mysterious maze.
But don't despair, even red-specked faces are not beyond repair,
For out of the blue comes green,
Out of sadness flowers dreams;
And even if one year before adult twenty,
You have not shaken off feelings of being forlorn and empty,
Paint a dream, and stick to it, but do not use glue,
For even dreams, like forgotten Elves, are not beyond the truth.

Jamie Lewis

My First Kiss

Oh when I think of my first kiss I shiver with delight
As he held me in the moonlight on a cold and frosty night
My toes all cold and tingling as I stood there in the snow
But his arms were wrapped around me and my heart was all aglow

So tall, so big. So handsome, with eyes all shining blue
I held my breath for words of love as my flame of passion grew
But no words came, just silence, had this love of mine gone dumb
Then his hand went in his pocket and he said, 'D'you want a gum.'

I'd never been in love before. Had I held my breath for this
Did he know that I was longing for my first romantic kiss
My knees they shook like jelly. My heart was very sad
But I picked a pretty green one. And sucked and sucked like mad.

I'd suffered all me curlers all through the blooming night
And put some cream and power on. Oh it really wasn't right
My gum was now all finished and I looked into his eyes
And then the magic happened, he had saved the big surprise.

He grabbed me by the shoulders, then his arms came round me tight
Then his lips came down all sticky. As he squeezed with all his might
Oh I thought I was in Heaven. Stars and bells attached my brain
Even though the taste was orange, Mother's warning was in vain.

Oh gosh how I recall that gum, the taste was so divine
As memories of it linger on, it sure did taste like wine
No future kiss has been the same, or sticky lips so sweet
And even now a pack of gums will make my poor heart bleat.

But alas I talk of yester-year, for today there's no such luck
For if history repeats itself, me teeth will get all stuck.

C Hall

Sweet Sixteen?

I well remember my first
Non-uniform day.
Dreading it.
I'm colour-blind
When it comes to clothes,
Paranoid about whispers.

I want to be popular.
What does that entail?
Should I smoke?
Renounce God?
Follow the crowd,
But upset my folks?

Why do parents never
Understand that you
Are trying to please
Both sides of the camp?
Should you tell them about
That little spot of bother at school?

Why are the teens
So confusing when,
Examining yourself in a mirror,
You ask what your identity
Should be?
A rebel, or a goody?

Decisions, decisions,
It's hard to decide.
There's no one to ask,
No place to hide
And that's why I hate
Being sixteen!
Lisa Foggo

Teenage Blues

I haven't got a boyfriend
'Cause my face is such a mess
Looks they say aren't everything
But help - I must confess

I've tried all kinds of different creams
To camouflage my face
But every day another spot
I'm running out of space

Why does it happen in your teens
It's puberty they say
Your body's going through a phase
It's changing every day

These teenage years are meant to be
The happiest in your life
So why am I so miserable
These spots give me some strife

The doctor's got a name for them
I think they call it acne
He says they'll go when I grow up
But when the hell will that be

Pauline R Simmons

Teenage Trials

Stolen kiss, first date,
Why did you come home so late?
Short skirt, parents frown,
Will you turn the music down?
Music hot, acne spots,
How much homework have you got?
Teachers moan, parents groan,
Please get off that telephone,
Messy gear, friends weird,
How I hate these teenage years,
When adulthood, I assume,
Will I get it right, like you?

Hazel Collins

Be Yourself

I used to know, or so I thought
What I wanted to be,
But as the years passed I realised
I just wanted to be me.

Free to do the things I want
When I want, and how,
Free to do what I want
Whenever I want, and now.

Not waiting for the time to pass
In some hour glass, or clock face,
But now while I'm young
And still part of the human race.

It would be nice to be
Famous or even rich,
And achieve or buy what I want
Without any hitch.

But to be yourself, yes just to be yourself
Is a real need,
The other things although quite nice
Are only greed.

So I'll carry on regardless
No matter what comes my way,
And just be content to be me
Every single day.

Jack Ellis

Exams

For five years I have sat and worked,
Now my brain is full to burst.
Everything I must now regurgitate.
Flippin' exams, just the word I hate.

Religious Studies on Monday morning
But revision is so boring.
Enthusiasm I've not got -
I sometimes think just stuff the lot.

I'm full of useless information
Ready for regurgitation.
Answer questions one after another,
Give me a break - I can't be bothered.

I've just got to carry on.
Six more then I'm on the run.
Freedom, I just can't wait.
But exams I flippin' hate.

I must now stop this rhyme
Or I will be out of time.
I've pages and pages of stuff to learn -
Then the whole flippin' lot I'm going to burn!

Emma J Palmer

An Empty Page

The pen of life writes on for you
Of new challenges and journeys too
Let's turn the page and have a look
At a clear fresh chapter in life's book

We packed your bags and shed a tear
But never when you might be near
We waved goodbye and forced a smile
As you joined the rank and file

A tidy room and a silent phone
Somehow it's strange not quite like home
No wet towels on the bathroom floor
No long haired youths leaning on the door

Time races on half term comes soon
Now you're here and oh that room
Loud music a pile of dirty clothes
That lies in a corner and just grows

But somehow now it's home again
And what we lost we also gain
Life and laughter comes flooding through
And we treasure the time we have with you

M Burgess

Teenage Woes

This mirror shows my true reflection,
Adonis longing for perfection.
Two hairs grow on my manly chest,
A-poking through my string-holed vest.
My greasy hair lies lank and limply,
My blotchy face is pocked and pimply.
I tried to shave the other day,
My nose kept getting in the way!
My singing voice, at one fell stroke,
Resembles, octaves down, a frog-like croak.
Not for me girlish invasion,
I'd never rise to the occasion!
My CD's, fortissimo, I'll play
And loll in bed the live-long day.
I'm gauche, I blush and go bright red,
I sometimes wish that I was dead.
I must take heart; it's true, you see,
There are many thousand youths like me!

Elizabeth Hardie

My First Kiss

Did you kiss? Asked my friend.
Oh yes it was awful
I couldn't wait for it to end.
It wasn't how I imagined
Like on the movie screen.
His lips were wet and slimy.
I really felt quite green.
I think I'll wait till I'm older
When I'll meet the man of my dreams
He'll kiss me oh so gently
Just like on the movie screens.

Dorothy Dawson

Growing Pains

I kissed him in the playground,
we kissed on the School Bus.
What did it really matter
that his face was oozing pus.
My friends will be green with envy
at my spotty beau,
we'll have interminable discussions
on how far I am prepared to go.

Sister Mary Monica says acne is a curse
sent to wicked boys from Heaven
and sometimes even worse.
She says kissing is quite sinful
but there is one thing worse than that
and that is eating food in public
whilst wearing your school hat.

I must admit she has me worried,
I might end up in hell.
Coz when I was kissing on the School Bus
I was chewing gum as well.

Pauline Brennan

Parenthood

When a tot is young it's mum mum mum,
Give me a bottle and change my bum.
Then comes the day you take them to school,
You think you have lost them once and for all.
They hold your hand tight crying 'Mummy don't go,'
So you stay a while until comfort they show.
Then comes the day they don't want you there,
They say 'Please don't collect me the children will stare.
They will think I'm a baby they will start to make fun,
I do love you Mummy but please don't come'.
Then comes the day their school days are through,
It's off to work, boyfriends too.
You sigh a big sigh 'What can I do,'
Just hope and pray the wisdom you fed,
Will help them from letting their heart rule their head.

V Eastwood

Yesterday's Teenager

The best years of my life
Were spent while in my teens
With cuban heels and pointed toes
And skin tight faded blue jeans
My hair was rather longer then
With sideburns down my cheeks
And spots that suddenly appeared
Always seemed to last for weeks
Girls would come a running
To my every beck and call
I really was a Jack the Lad
In fact I knew it all
My music was the noisy kind
That my parents just couldn't stand
But I knew the words of every song
And every singer in every band
My car it was a banger
But like a star I could be seen
As I drove around the town all night
I felt just like James Dean
Now the young folks of today
Who moan about being alive
Will one day be the same as me
A yesterday's teenager, aged forty-five.

Tony Hayden

The Dreaded Spot

God no not another
I won't be able to face
My brother,

He's bound to tease
And try to squeeze,

The more I look it
Seems to grow
It even has a subtle glow,

I can't go out today
Unless it fades away,

I could use my sister's
Concealer that might make
It pale,

Please make it go away God
I start to wail,

Claudia Sidebottom won't
Kiss me again with this
Upon my chin,

Oh dear God what a predicament
I'm in,

I expect you've guessed by now
What I've got
Yes that's right the dreaded
Spot.

Lynn Barnes

Our Daughter

We have a daughter
Nearly grown up at ten plus three
Ann is her given name
A comely lass is she
I can't say she's beautiful
Though she is fair of face
She has a figure problem
All in a certain place
She has dainty hands and dainty feet
Nice eyes and nose and lips
The top half of her is passable
The trouble is her hips
Some would say she's buxom
Others that she's fat
I only know we love her
And that I think is that!

Plover

A Teenager's Life

A teenagers life is.
Getting up the nerve to ask that girl to dance,
at the school disco.
Battling the spots that form regiments across the
battle field of your face.
And praying you get those fashion jeans,
Instead of those black semi flares.

A teenagers life is.
Having to share a bedroom with your little brother,
Who finds and shows Mum the magazine you got from
Jimmy Tomkins in form 4C.
Taking those exams that you wished you had revised for,
That first french kiss, that took your breath away.

Feeling the happiness with your girlfriend,
Arguing with Dad, over that 10.30 curfew.

The excitement of your first sexual experience,
And the feelings that it brought.
And finally starting work,
Your first wages, and coming home tired out.
That's what a teenagers life is all about.

A L Barlow

Kiss From Maggie

The day I saw Maggie
Her hair as red as gold
Walking so sure footed in the snow
I followed her step by step
Until she reached the farm
I said 'Oh! Maggie Maggie
I love you so please give me a kiss.'
She turned her big brown eyes twinkling
'You may have a kiss Duncan lad
When all your spots have gone'
I ran down the hill
Rubbing snow on my face
I must have looked a terrible disgrace
But lo and behold when I looked in the mirror
My spots had gone like the wind
I ran up the hill shouting
'Maggie oh Maggie
I claim my kiss
My spots have gone and I have grown.'
Maggie's kiss was my delight
And will be for the rest of my life

Erimar MacMillian

Gazing

Whoever invented the mirror?
I do wish that they had not.
For whenever I gaze in the mirror,
I find yet another spot!

It wasn't there last evening;
I'm sure there were only four,
red and angry and heaving.
Please - I don't want any more.

My brother's face is smooth and clear,
no blemishes to be seen;
he's older than me by a couple of years.
Where the hell is that spot cream!

Mum says I musn't squeeze them,
I'll only make things worse.
So I peer and finger and poke them;
and all I can do is curse.

How will I find a girlfriend,
when I look such a dreadful sight?
Covered in acne is hardly a trend;
she'll think I'm infested with blight!

I'm praying the years will pass quickly;
by then the spots will have cleared.
Now - to stop me looking so sickly,
I think I'll just grow a beard.

Julie Newsum

Zits!

Zits are big, zits are small,
But I wish I had no zits at all.
Big and red and oozing slime,
More erupting all the time!
Like volcanoes, zits can spew
Lots of pus and greasy goo.
You rub on tubes and tubes of cream;
Wake up every day and scream;
'It's not fair the way they sprout!
Out, darn spot! Darn spot get out!'
Still there isn't any hope,
Though you use ten bars of soap,
Nothing works, so on your head
You use a paper bag, instead!

Robert Houghton

Boyfriends

My first was a lad with orange hair
Brushed stiff and spiky, coated with gel,
One half orange, one half blue,
Looked pretty like a peacock,
Like a lavatory brush - well -

Dad disappeared inside the tool shed,
Mum sucked her cheeks and scuttled away,
But he'd put on his clean art-frayed jeans,
Laced up his trainers, polished his earrings,
He knew some funny jokes - anyway -

My next was a lover of *heavy metal*,
We twanged his twelve-string guitar till late,
Dad thumped the ceiling and took to drink,
We raced home at dawn on his motorbike,
He was a groovy dancer - great -

Then there was Ricky with his mountain bike,
He could swoop up the rockery and spin in the air,
Really go for *wheelies* on Dad's front lawn,
Leap over bushes and the garden fence,
We went on track rides - everywhere -

The neighbours got moody and put up gates,
Dad locked the car away, rescued the cat,
Mum tied chains and posts round the rose beds,
I thought the boys had *character* -
What's wrong with that?

Esme Francis

Spots

Oh God I've got another one,
all red and round and glowing,
there's not much room left on my face,
and I'm sure this spot's still growing,

I've tried all the creams and lotions,
that promise a spot free face,
but I think this spot knows all the tricks,
and I'm losing in this race.

I used to be quite popular,
things used to be so simple,
until the day I woke to find,
my face was one big pimple.

I don't go out much anymore,
I prefer to be alone,
and if I get the urge to talk,
there's always the telephone.

My Mother says they will clear up,
one day they'll go away,
so I'll stay close to a mirror,
and wait for that wonderful day.

Walter McGoff

Journey to Eternity

I am a lone adventurer,
On a ten year quest,
I will leave an innocent,
The experience I gain will shape me,
For life,
I am aboard the ship I'll sail,
Bound for the sea of eternity,
Part of a huge, never ending fleet,
Following in the wake of others,
Struggling to hold the wheel,
Which swings wildly,
Crashing on through the rocks,
Out into the deeper ocean,
Away from home,
Will I encounter winds? Rain?
Creatures of the deep?
Pain, loneliness or sorrow?
Company, happiness or joy?
Or will my engine fail?
And I drift aimlessly, going nowhere?

Mark Eaton

Their Own Future

Teenagers have always had problems.
They're ever betwixt and between.
No longer are they little children
who shouldn't be heard, only seen.
They have adjustments to make
until they become *grown up*
and everyone knows there is many
a slip between lip and the cup.
They're faced with so many pressures
from folk who would lead them astray,
but most of our wonderful teenagers
come through at the end of the day.
Teenagers need our encouragement.
Be entrusted to do things right.
They are, after all, their own future
so they *have* to get things right.

Mavis Fox

Up and Away

When I was yet a teenage boy.
Flushed high in laughter, youth, and joy
Each dawn arrived in sunshine mood -
Each evening blushed in gratitude.
Bright promise challenged me each day
To life enriched with *up and away*.

Fortunes were there for me to make;
Adventures there to undertake,
Doorways open; the world a dare -
Thresholds to cross to anywhere.
All this and more, much more, was mine
If I faced up to the task some time.

Did I get there? The answer: *no*;
I monkeyed with my life, and so
When it came to winning, then I
Was never one to qualify.
In truth I never won because
I played the fool like the fool I was.

Due time has marched and life moves on -
The last of gravy trains has gone.
But now, for me, it matters not,
I put up with the lot I've got.
My only sorrow to this day:
I missed out on that *up and away*.

John Castel-Nuovo

Spots

Spots are only funny when they're other people's spots,
They spread across your features like fluorescent polka-dots.

Completely unexpected, they erupt when it is dark,
With grim determination to create a blotchy mark!

Go near them with your fingers and they always seem to know,
The more you try to squeeze them, the angrier they grow.

And just when you are going out they'll choose to have a race,
See how fast they can multiply, and cover up your face!

The thought of people noticing can fill your heart with dread,
You'd like to put a massive paper bag over your head.

But next time someone points them out just smile and grit your teeth.
It's not the spots that matter, it's the person underneath!

Debbie Cowdry

Feelings of a Depressed Teenager

I'm sixteen, so what,
I feel angry and blue,
I feel depressed, but why?
I don't have a clue.
It's dragging me down,
I can't take anymore
Just leave me alone
It's my own private war.
I don't understand it,
I just want to cry,
I feel more desolate,
As each day goes by.
I feel so closed in,
Can't set myself free,
I've given up trying,
What's happening to me?
It seems never ending,
Like time has stood still,
I want to be happy,
Perhaps one day I will.

Sheila Chugg

The Unwashed Masses of the Younger Generation

The word *teenager* cringes me out -
And before you inform me of my poor English
I'd like to add that I am seventeen years old
And therefore exempt from all blame.
The education system, after all, is not what it was.
As I am constantly reminded, my nine GCSE's
Are facile and useless,
And that as a product of the Twentieth Century
I have no morals or compassion for others.
I don't have to walk ten miles to school in a sack,
So am therefore unaware of human suffering.
When I leave what I'm told is my poor excuse for a school,
With what I'm told are my pseudo qualifications,
I won't have to work down 't pit
And swallow coal for twelve hours a day.
I won't have to break my back shifting firewood,
Or suffer the Terrible Winter of '45
In an unheated shack in North Yorkshire.
I'm told that I've never had it so good.
I may become one of the three million unemployed,
Get evicted from my council flat
And spend the rest of my life
In a cardboard box outside Woolworth's -
But then I would be typically audacious
To consider this at all comparable.
I am, after all, one uncouth lout among millions.

Emma Brockes (17)

First Date

In the moth eaten stalls,
Attempting to be mesmerized by the screen,
They sit.
Nervously unsure of the others intentions,
Elbow to elbow
And yet, worlds apart,
They feel like Columbus, setting foot on new ground.
Sexuality is unexplored, but land has been found.

Kevin J Moloney

Bra!

My Mum thought it best
Now I am bigger
To disregard my vest
And wear a bra instead
How I hate it so
Frilly, itchy bra
Elasticated straps
Leaving indentations
It looks so stupid
And doesn't quite fit
Without cotton-wool
Stuffed inside it
Still, Mum knows best
(I suppose)
But I much preferred
My old vest

Tina Gale

Ambition

He wished that he was sexy,
He wished that he was good.
He wished with all his little heart,
That Maisie Fellows would.

He'd dined her in his little home,
On new brown bread and coffee.
On chicken legs and pâté,
And home made treacle toffee.

She was his unattainable,
His harbinger of plenty.
His dart that never would land,
Into the treble twenty.

Until that fateful day she did,
And he found that he couldn't.
Then he wished with all his little heart,
That Maisie Fellows wouldn't.

D T Baker

Teenage Strife

Teenage explosion of explicit emotions,
daubing walls with reckless motions.
Meaningless gangs rending their fury,
on life's innocent jury.

Razor blade minds with cutting tongues,
where silence belongs.
Futile hope in decaying world,
where starvation is the final word.

Fighting talk of distraught youth,
whose clenched fist seems so uncouth.
Another generation lost,
at whose cost?

Lost goals of growing up,
no reason for the empty cup.
Teenage explosion of explicit anger,
no way out is the real danger.

David Buck

Changes

Baggy jeans, denim shirts,
Leather jackets, mini skirts.
Let's be trendy, let's be cool,
We're the ones who want to rule.
Pierce our noses, shave our heads,
Let us sleep long in our beds.
Ban the bomb, don't eat the meat,
Knock the government off their feet.
Dance away the night to rave,
No one tells us to behave.
Leaving school, I just can't wait,
To be the other side of the gate.
Money's scarce, can't get a job,
Mum and Dad call me a yob.
My friends don't call me any more,
I think it is because I'm poor.
I didn't study well at school,
I used to love playing the fool.
I've grown the hair back on my head,
I get up early from my bed.
I be polite to Mum and Dad,
I've realised now that I was bad.
Now is the time to make things right,
No longer do I start a fight.
Instead I'll do the best I can,
Now I have grown into a man.

Patricia Slatter

Adolescence

Living with Adolescence is hell.
Being a parent to this is as well.
Having a lad of sixteen,
arguments obscene,
times are lean.

Spots and acne everywhere.
The teenager argues without any care.
Everything's wrong.
He doesn't belong.
He starts to pong.

Changes of mood, up and down.
Facial and body hair now are found.
What torment
to parents is sent.
Anger is spent.

Growing up is a painful time.
Emotions mixed up by design.
Soon hope this will end.
I'll go round the bend.
Help will you send?
Or I'll pack a suitcase and leave!

L Knight

Hairhead

Why do hairdressers never cut your hair
In the way that you ask?
Is it such an effort,
Such a Herculean task, to
Give you what you want
And made you look
Like the photograph
In the book that you bring her?

All you want's to be a diva
Or a torch-song singer,
To be like Cindy Crawford
In this month's Vogue,
Madonna, Cher, or Kylie Minogue.
She doesn't understand
You're a star in the mirror
Singing with hairbrush in hand,
But she wields the scissors
And risks your career by
Jeopardising your image
And just missing your ear.

Angela White

Sorry

Darling, I'm sorry, I left you,
Sorry , I said, 'I don't care!'
I long for your love and devotion,
Unhappy, and full of despair.

Each night and day I am lonely,
No one is there, when I cry;
Please tell me, that you feel the same way,
So lonely, you wish you could die.

It's worth the try, just you and I,
For a new hope to discover.
I love you still, I always will,
Because we were meant for each other.

Darling, please say, 'I'm forgiven,'
Love that is true, cannot die,
Forget all my foolish emotion,
I'm sorry, that I made you cry.

Cyril Carter

First Date

What time are yer meeting 'er?
Quarter to eight.
Well don't get there early,
It's cool to be late.

And if she don't turn up
Just play it real natural,
Act dead unconcerned,
And all matter of factual.

Do yer think that she won't then,
I'll feel a right twit!
And 'int this my luck,
I've come out in a zit!

'Ave I put too much spray on
She might think it's naff,
I don't want 'er to think
I'm just good for a laugh

Can you lend us a tenner
In case I run out.
I'd be right embarrassed
If I got caught out.

Wot about this new shirt,
Does it go with the shoes,
Where d'ya think we should go
Or should I let her choose

Will she fancy me loads,
and let me french kiss her,
Hey it's seven, I'm off now
I don't want to miss 'er!

Jessica Smith

Oh!

Oh! What is happening to me?
I've heard they call it puberty.
My legs keep growing, overnight!
My trousers always seem too tight.
I hit my head on the car door
where I always used to fit before.
My voice keeps coming out all wonky,
Sometimes like me, others like a donkey!
My face is filling up with zits
and there's hair upon my naughty bits.
When I see girls my thoughts just race
especially when they smile in my face.
I don't know how long this time will last
but the sooner it ends won't be too fast!

Maggie Doré

I Was One

I went to school half heartedly
Wrote down my thoughts in a diary,
Could not really make it out,
What these teenage years were
all about,
We had our heart aches,
Big and small,
Mother did not understand at all,
The first boyfriend broke my heart,
I never thought that we would part,
Off my food, spots appeared,
Oh, was love so very dear,
Cigarettes, yes I did try,
Played truant, it was the style,
Stayed out late, tried the beer,
But I came through these teenage
years,
A little wiser in many ways,
I am still learning every day.

Pauline Crossland

Father Said

Father said, 'Bring him to tea.'
My sisters remarked, 'Rather you than me.'
Michael and I had been going steady
Father said, 'You're not ready.'
'Not ready?' I asked, looking blank
'No!' said Father, 'I'm being quite frank.'
'Not ready?' I repeated, going bright red.
'No,' said Father. 'Put it out of your head.'
Does he mean marriage, I thought
He wouldn't be easily caught!

I waited for Michael at the front gate,
He said that the bus was very late.
The time arranged was half past three,
Father didn't like waiting for tea.
Boyfriends invited, should be on time,
We girls always had to toe the line.
Tea was not a success, I might say
And I remember it well, to this very day.
Needless to say, wedding bells didn't chime,
As Father said, 'There was plenty of time.'

Things might have been different, I agree
If only Michael hadn't come to tea.
Father could dampen any girls chances,
Nipping in the bud a suitor's advances.
He didn't like Michael's attitude
But I felt very little gratitude.
My heart was broken many times
Before I heard wedding bell chimes.
The young men were brave indeed
Who entered our house, for a hand to plead!

Patricia Emery

What Did You Do Today

What did you do at school, dear?
Nothing, I hear you say.
The amount of nothing you seem to do
Would fill a book, with some over too
And yet I know that this isn't true
Your marks give you away.

Have you finished your homework?
I don't have any, you say.
So just when do you do your work?
Your teachers say you do not shirk,
So in the library you must lurk
While others are at play.

Where are you going tonight, dear?
Nowhere, I hear you say.
Only around to my mate, John,
If I don't hurry, he'll be gone
There's a teenage disco at the Swan.
God keep you safe, I pray.

One day, long into future time,
Mother, I'll hear you say.
My kids won't tell me what I should know
About their friends or where they go.
Was I that awful? It didn't seem so.
You certainly were, I'll say.

F Russell

Growing Pains

Trying, testing teenage years,
fraught with fears and tears.
Striving, oh so hard to cope,
to face the future with new hope.

The world out there is cruel and hard,
constantly we're on guard.
Exams and jobs and parents, too,
of all our problems these are few.

Beneath our *nonchalant* air,
we really need to know you care.
To be there - yet - to let us go,
on life's see-saw - to and fro.

The highs and lows of life we face,
and try to keep our step apace.
By our mistakes we have to learn,
realise, amend and so discern.

These awesome years they will not last,
in other moulds we will be cast.
Now grown, adult, and quite mature,
for life's arena - to endure,

M P Johnson

I Love to Kiss

Sweet sixteen I love to kiss
At least full on the lips
Boys they seem real silly
It's enough to make you sick.

They fumble in their pockets
Then kiss me on the cheek
It seems to me they're a little bit slow
Too meek and mild, too weak

I always make the first move
Look up into their eyes
Place my arms around their shoulders
Pretending to be a little bit shy

I love to kiss long and tender
Passionately, I would say
One kiss from me will guarantee
They'll return for more next day!

M E Wickett

Bully Boys

The school day has ended, everyone has gone home
Except me, I'm still in the playground alone
I feel sick and afraid for I've no cash to give away
To the boys who bully and taunt me each day

They will be waiting for me at the end of the street
I've done them no harm, and there is no need to treat
Me the way that they do, they tear at my clothes
Calling me names as I ward off the blows

I can't tell my Mum, she will go and complain
She'll speak to the Teacher and I can't stand the strain
It will make matters worse, it has happened before
My life is so miserable, I don't like school any more

C R Maggs

Parents - Who Would Have Them?

Their language is strange
I cannot understand their aim,
I offer to wash the dishes
I listen to all their wishes,
And when Sinatra sings out
Shut up! I try not to shout,
I listen to all their problems
Sit down and talk I tell them.

Dad's haircut can be so square
I try not to blush when friends stare,
His clothes so drab and lifeless
I find it hard to understand I confess,
They come home at weird times
Catch me watching the news at nine,
Parents who would have them?

Mum insists on the hat so black
The assistant smiles I'm taken aback
Looks like a granny before her time
But you cannot change her mind,
They always know the best
My advice is not given the test,
That old dress is it still in fashion?
Dad thinks it still looks smashing.

David Tyrrell

Unemployment

I wake up in the morning,
But there's nothing much to do.
I reach to turn the telly on
With my snooker cue.
And here are Richard and Judy
Presenting their daily show.
Afraid it's really not my scene,
So back to sleep I go.

I get up in the afternoon,
But there's nothing much to do.
I raid the fridge for things to eat
Then raid the cupboards too.
I read the local paper,
From the front page to the back.
Then turn again to the half page
Of situations vac.

I scan the advertisements,
With an ease borne of despair.
Not expecting anything
And pretending I don't care.
Then suddenly my eye alights
On the job just made for me.
I reach for pen and paper
And make my silent plea.

Sally Childress

I Remember it Well

I remember my first kiss, it still tickles me to bits,
He took me to the cinema the big one called *The Ritz.*
Well, to put you in the picture, I'd ne'er been kissed before
And the first time that he asked me I ran in and slammed the door.
It's not that I just didn't want, it's just that I was shy,
And I thought, *If he don't ask again I'll just curl up and die.*
I used to wonder if he would and I wondered if I'd like,
And then one night he asked again and I said, 'Get on your bike!'
It's not that I was frigid or anything like that
It's just I thought that once you kissed you started getting fat.
There's no two ways about it I was scared the stork would come
'Cos no one ever told me that a bairn grew in your tum.
So I daren't let him kiss me and he got awful mad,
I almost let him once or twice but I thought of my old Dad.
Well, years went by and he got wed and then his wife she died,
I married him soon after and no kisses were denied.
Now we've been married sixty years and still kiss with lots of passion
Not like the early days gone by when my kisses were on ration.

Euphemia McKillop

First Date

Hair all coiled into a pleat
Nails manicured, feeling neat.
Petticoat starched, with flouncy frill,
Feeling really dressed to kill.
Gliding gently down the stairs,
As my new beau has just appeared.
Just seventeen, and life's a ball,
Now I'm ready in the hall.
Clock ticks by, almost eight,
This is my first grown up date.
Lecture over from Mum last night,
Be home by ten, to do it right.
So by the arm I'm proudly led,
Not forgetting what Ma had said.
Dancing in the village hall,
Watching the clock I can recall.
Not daring to assume my fate,
If not at ten, by the garden gate.
No sooner thought than like Cinderella
I trek for home with my sweet fellah,
Looking back it seemed not bold,
Doing then as I was told.
Time has since then rolled away,
Married with daughters I now say,
Don't be late home. Oh! The echoes I hear,
It's not so long since
yester-year.

Eve Adams

God Give Me Strength - The Plea of a Teenager's Mum

For Pete's sake, turn down that din,
Drives me mad, when I walk in.
Do they call it heavy-metal,
Sounds like banging on a kettle.
Nothing like it, in my day,
I am very pleased to say.

I'd be crazy to presume,
That you'd vacc'd and cleaned your room.
How long were you on the 'phone?
I have every right to moan.
When he sees the bill come through,
Dad will say 'I'm soft with you.'

Can't afford designer-gear,
We're not made of money here.
Why d'you never wear a dress,
Jeans with cuts are such a mess.
You're in trouble. You just swore.
Don't march out and slam the door.

Who's the boy, who made a date?
Come straight home. Please don't be late.
I don't really like your crowd,
They seem arrogant and loud.
I know, you don't give two hoots,
You're too big to fit your boots.

Teenagers make me feel ill,
Wished I'd stayed upon the pill.
They're as selfish as can be.
All they think is *Me, me, me.*
Mine's a trial, at times, I know.
Wonder why I love her so.

Margaret Myttion

Try to Remember

Tidy your bedroom again you say
Do something with your hair
How can you go out just looking like that?
It seems that you really don't care
You say this day after day to me
Oh I wish you'd remember one thing
You probably were the same as me
Before my Dad gave you a ring
Haven't you finished your homework?
And where do you think you've been?
Who was that boy I saw you with?
Don't you care what the neighbours have seen?
Oh Mum I wish you could see it
The way that I do today
It's not that I'm trying to rebel against you
I just need to do things my way

T Hennessey

Teenage Blues

My Mum and Dad said the other day
As *teenagers* their life was riotous in every way!
I really wonder when? As they had to be home by half-past ten!
When I borrow Mum's make-up my face goes all blotchy and red,
And my Dad says 'Try soap and water instead.'
I wish I looked like *Trish* in *Take the High Road!*
Then I'd have *boyfriends* by the load!
But I'm skinny, straight haired and have to wear *specs*!
So I guess I'm just one of nature's *social wrecks*
At the school disco I dreamed of romance!
But my escort from *next door* couldn't even dance!
That was the night I got my first *goodnight kiss!*
Something I'd recommend anyone to miss!
For on his teeth his wore braces!
A rotteweiller could not have made any worse faces!
A kiss from him wouldn't make me kick over the traces!
Yes! A teenager's life has many such disgraces!

Flora Divers

First Date

She had a date with curly hair
She was on time and he was there
When they had met was he that small?
Lolling lazily by the wall

His jaws chewed busily on the gum
Kissing would not be much fun
But a date was a date, the first she'd had
Perhaps it would not be too bad

'Hi kid,' he said? Where was his grammar?
She cringed inside, could only stammer
'I'm not a kid, don't call me that.'
Her one desire to leave him flat

But teenage pride must make a stand
So, playing the part, she took his hand
Into a small cafe to eat, he took her to a window seat
Sitting there for all to see, the nasty way he supped his tea

No fluttering heart beating strong, the magazines must all be wrong
She'd tell the girls when she got home that she would rather be alone

Doreen Gardner

Life - Begins at Forty!

'Put your things away,' says Mum
'Tidy up your room.'
'What,' I say, 'You know I can't,
I'm going out at noon,
I've got a spot I have to squeeze
My hair, it is a mess
I must do something about my nails
And press my shirt or dress.
Who's seen my tights, where can they be
I thought I put them down
On the bookcase in the hall,
Becky, you can frown.
A phone call now, for me, you say
Please, tell Jim I'm not in,
How can I talk to him today
I'm going out with Glyn.
Oh, now my finger nail has split
I'll have to patch it up,
Tea, no Mum, I haven't got time,
Not even for one cup.
Who said the teenage years were fun
With so much going wrong -
Danny, turn the radio up,
I want to hear that song;
Mum, these kids, they drive me mad
Can't they come downstairs
They touch my things and just annoy,
Can I see some grey hairs!
Who wants a brother who's a pain,
A sister who's so naughty
Perhaps I'll skip a few years by
And start my life at forty!'

Wendy A Cudd

Halfway . . .

I wasn't old enough they said,
While others said, *too young*.
I've got a lot to learn it seems in all the years to come.
But as I built some knowledge then few things went right for me,
The books were just too hard to read, the films I couldn't see.
Too young for bars, too old for toys,
Few things were very easy.
Still tied to go to school each day with dreams I went quite crazy.
Still at fourteen what can you do . . . ?
The world is not so kind,
As I'll some day say to my son,
Whose dreams may follow mine.

Paul Sanders

Late Night?

I am not coming home till half past ten
I'll die, my friends will all make fun of me.
No one else will have to be in by then.

I'm sick and tired of who? What? Where? And when?
I want some space and I need to be free
I am not coming home till half past ten.

You think that all I think about is men.
I don't know why I couldn't have a key.
No one else will have to be in by then.

We're all just friends. Pardon? Is who called Ben?
I believe there is someone called Ben. We. . .
I am not coming home till half past ten.

You're the only one. Phone any of them.
Please. I'll clean my room tomorrow, you'll see.
No one else will have to be in by then.

Well I know Sam's got to be in by ten.
And Lisa said nine? She would wouldn't she?
I am not coming home till half past ten,
No one else will have to be in by then.

Sue Smith

Farewell Punch and Judy

Don't book me up a seaside holiday
I'll stay at home alone while you're away
Growing every day see how tall I am
The label, size M means that I'm a man
The homework will be done night after night
I'll feed the dog so he don't go and bite
The Milkman will be paid dead on the dot
And the dust will be removed as a job lot
The cans will all be saved to help the world
And I will see that none of them are hurled

They will be no stagnant socks in the linen bin
And thankfully this year, creases are *In*
Two whole weeks without making me bed
Well, it's more important that the cat is fed
I'll bring the bike in! For inspection
As it's usually met with rejection
I'll phone around, invite a few mates
We'll eat out of the paper, forget about plates
I hope *they* get up early to go on their way
So I can start my first Home Holiday

Maureen Barrett

First Kiss

An innocent kiss
of divine bliss,
Sweet deceit entangled
in the young.

Hearts racing
while they're embracing,
They bond with
eternal youth.

A heated passion
of the fashion,
Seasoned by the swirls
of first love.

Amanda Reason

Growing Up

It wasn't easy being a little girl
With the world so big it made my head whirl
A tiny tot in a land of giants
A little girl to play amongst the plants
Someone to hide behind Mummy's skirt
Big brown eyes that would learn to flirt
School time was a time to learn
Whilst nerves made my stomach churn
I started off bottom of the class
But I improved and shone quite fast
At thirteen it was time for boys
A fair exchange for my old toys
But with the boys came exams and spots
And thick make-up that went into clots
Most teenager years were rather fun
A time for holidays and lots of sun
I'd come a long way from that little girl
Who found the world so big, it make her head whirl.

Cherry Somers-Dowell

Parents

My parents say they love me,
But only when I'm good.
A subjective, conditional love,
Received, if I just would.
There never is a time
When I feel their love is free.
So they will never see or feel
That being that is me.

Josephine Blyth

First Date

I am a teenager on my first date
Trying to cover a pimpled face,
'Mum, I can't go like this,' was the cry,
'If he sees me I would die.'
So with powder and rouge
I tried to conceal
Those ugly old spots
So better I'd feel.
With Mum's help and persuasion
I put on plenty of foundation
And so with that base
I looked upon a new face.
'That's much better,' Mum declared,
'Now there is no need to be scared.'
'What if he wants a kiss?' I said,
'That is the moment I most dread.'
'Just let him have a peck, don't fight
And quickly say, that's it, goodnight.'

A Saunders

First Love

'Meet me by the bridge,' he said in husky voice,
Passing quickly and with reddening face
Was out of sight, eager to race away
From me he longed to meet.

I blushed and would have answered yes,
But he was gone, and I was left
With thumping heart and quite bereft
Of thinking clearly, just the bridge remained.

As I approached, a shadowy form
Stretched out upon the grassy bank
Rose quickly, and with outstretched hands
Reached out to me shyly, without a word.

E Joyce Lock

Sea Change

Breach the gap of generation,
Damn torrential expectation,
Rollercoasting deafening breakers,
Grab the thrills, the spills, be takers,
Thundering waves below to hide,
Tender sensitive inside.

Cast adrift with limpets clinging,
Sebaceous ocean seaweed bringing
Confiscation of free will,
Unfettered growth salt cannot still,
Buffeted urchins now collected,
All sounds familiar neglected.

Search until the shoal is found,
Gaining depth, dark, where Man is drowned,
Without a backward glance or wave
Bright fish are found, he is their slave.
For one full season till its wain,
His desperate wish, acceptance gain.

With Summer seas so turns the tide,
Calmer waters opening wide
To warm lagoons and tranquil shore,
And self destructive thoughts no more
Pervade his every wakening move,
He is sea changed, his worth has proved.

Sheila Payton

Tongue Tied

I met a vixen in the woods
And she was running wild,
With red-brown hair
Blue eyes that stare
And almost not a child.

I wanted to ask her home for tea
To show that I was kind,
But all I did was stand and stare
And give a sheepish smile.

If I see her again one day
I'll not let her get away,
Persuasive words I'll find to say
That will make her want to stay,
Quite unlike
The first time.

David Madeira-Cole

A Mother's Lament

The pretty daughter we once knew,
Has joined a loud-mouthed teenage crew,
Her hair is pink, her eyelids black,
Her clothes are shapeless as a sack.
She brings home friends from far and near,
They strut around in leather gear,
Made up like clowns, with laughs and hoots,
They tramp upstairs with clumping boots.
Turn up the noise. 'Music,' she says,
And chatters loudly as it plays.
Then suddenly it's time to fly,
They rush outside and pass me by,
She kisses me, I sigh, 'Have fun.'
The teenage years have just begun!

Isobel MacCallum

Party Game

Tonight after the party, I pray he'll walk me home.
Bet he smells delicious, the sexiest cologne.
At school I'm forever watching, yet often with some pain.
He stoops, reties his undone shoelace, moth-like I crave the flame.
Skin glossy brown as any chestnut, hair dark as secret cave.
I tell myself, I'll say *hello*, but know I'm not that brave.
I shut my eyes and think about, his sculptured silhouette.
So real, his wine-like-tasting kisses, his lips of smooth velvet.
Now here, in brand new party dress, and playing Postman's Knock.
He's waiting for me in the hall, I'm in a state of shock.
Wide eyes brightening, body shivering, delightful innocent dread.
That boy whose carefully chosen number, controls my heart and head.
Door closed, words, hang uneasy between us, his winning smile, and wink.
I breathe in paradise so longed for, sharp smell, eyes smart, I blink.
He moves towards me, his lips puckering, I whisper, 'I feel sick.'
His clammy hand grabs mine, I blurt, 'Yyy. . .uck, you smell of *Vick*.'

Pamela Pitts

Seventeen

Ten years ago this poet was still only seventeen,
And struggling with razors and shaving cream,
I had a few spots which shone red and bright,
I would stare in the mirror at this awful sight,
Using the special creams I tried to make them go away,
But they only stung my face and all the spots would stay,
It was around this time that I discovered the opposite sex,
But when I found a girlfriend I didn't know what happened next,
Even holding hands was hard for me to do,
It was little wonder kissing was a problem too,
At school I was in the sixth form and doing an extra year,
But my interest was in pubs and drinking lots of beer,
Homework held little appeal for me, so I would plug in my guitar,
My sixth form life was drifting by and I wasn't getting far,
Then the exam dates got closer so I worked with sudden haste,
Not wanting my extra year to have been all a total waste,
Eventually the results came through and some were pretty good,
But I hadn't really worked as hard as perhaps I should,
So here I was in the big wide world and feeling all alone,
Looking ahead with mixed emotions as if I'd just left home,
It was time to go and find a job, but what did I want to do?
This was all unclear in my mind and I didn't have a clue,
One by one I applied for jobs, but it all seemed pretty bleak,
I found in the end a YTS place but only stayed for a week,
Once again I was out of work, but it wasn't all doom and gloom,
Good times were up ahead, it was my eighteenth birthday soon!
In writing this rambling poem, I have reflected on that time,
The seventeenth year of my life preserved as a page of rhyme. . .

Stephen Norris

Growing Pains

Spotty face and puppy fat
Puberty and moods
Hiding in your bedroom
Seeking solitude.

Nose too small - bum too big
Bosom, non-existent
Being chased by teenage boys
Whose patter is persistent.

Stuffing hankies down your bra
Feeling shy and awkward
Giggle, blush and feel a fool
When *bust* starts falling downwards!

At last the teens are over
The twenties are most welcome
My bust has grown, and spots are gone
My moods are few and seldom.

What's this I see? - Oh damn! Oh blast!
A big, enormous blackhead!
Instead of going out tonight
I'll hide beneath my bedspread!

Marjorie C Edgar

Youth of Today

It's hard to be a teenager,
In these days of violence and crime,
They find that people criticise,
And blame them, half the time.
Nothing they do, seems to be right,
No matter how hard they try,
They're suspected of being a fighter; a drunkard;
Or drugged up to the eyes.

A rotten minority gives Youth a bad name,
And fingers point and accuse,
You only have to read the paper,
Or hear it on the news.
But what about the lasses and lads,
Who lend a helping hand,
To raise funds for the unfortunates,
Of this sick and depraved land?

There's many a teenager who's given his time,
To help the poor and needy,
They're not all hooligans, louts and thugs,
Selfish, rough or greedy.
So don't be hasty, in your judgement,
Of the teenagers of today,
Be fair, and give them half a chance, -
They *know* crime doesn't pay.

Sue Wingett

Teenage Venom

**Here comes that awful Samantha Clare,
She thinks she's the answer to every boys prayer,
Doesn't she look a dreadful sight
Plastered with make-up and her jeans far too tight?
Don't bother with her, she's a spiteful bitch,
Well, she is, or I am, - I'm not sure which.**

Nancy Sheldon

Fine Feathers

When I'm sixteen I'll be beautiful
like a swan
I'll wear a full flare fluorescent
skirt with white penny spots
sprays of can-can nylon lace will
foam where I walk
a wash of pink
a wake of green
and there will be something
inside my bra.

When the jukebox plays
my head will be as high as
spinning stars
I will glide with pointy-toed
pearlized poise
gracefully holding the impossible
glass cups of espresso
without splashing
and my saucer will not hold drips
I'll leave no trail where I have been
except pink lipstick prints
and the soft touch of fine feathers.

June P Portlock

First Love

Mom please lift the curfew for me
it's my very first dance Saturday
I will be with my friends until the dance ends
so please lift the curfew for me
oh gosh, I've got some spots on my face
now I'll look an awful disgrace
the girls will all giggle and stare
the boys will pretend I'm not there
why now must these spots mark my face
I'll say I'm ill and won't go
but that I'll regret I just know
I'll try make-up and stuff to cover them up,
and hope it's so dark they won't show
this day has come real quick
I'm so nervous I feel sick
for I know he'll be there
the one with the lovely black hair
in the clothes that are always so slick
that's the third dance, I've sat out alone
I really wish I'd stayed home
my he's walking my way, what shall I say
I best quickly tidy my hair with my comb
I feel like I'm walking on air
I know now he really does care
'cos he's walked me home to my gate
he's asked me out on a date
we've sealed our first kiss
to me this was sheer bliss
and to see him again I can't wait.

Patricia Barr

Duty Calls

The room is stiflingly hot,
The television is on,
A hazy jumble of words and images in my peripheral mind.
No one listens to it.
They sit and gaze into the past, reliving their lives;
Or nod awkwardly against their seat.
Beyond the mumbling television
The plastic flowers hang dull and dusty
In the conservatory
Their colours false and scent pretended.
Beyond that glowers the granite-grey Cornish sky
Over the brown hills.
Beyond that again lies the merciless, turbulent Atlantic Ocean.
The cheerful walls and pretty paintings seem
To me a mockery of the inhabitants
Who are bleached and faded by contrast.
A wizened woman wakes from her trance,
Calls out for her brother shrilly.
A warden hurries over to pacify her
Whispering to me confidingly, 'She lost him in the war, you know.'
At last Mum finishes her one-sided conversation
The endless half-hour is over.
The door shuts behind me.
I leap and run
Glad to be free,
And energetic,
And young.

Kiran Harvey

The Generation Gap. . .

Listen to me Mother; listen to me Father;
Help me to understand the chaos all around.
Give me a chance Mother; give me a chance Father;
It isn't all my fault, that I don't understand.
I need to develop my own mind; and my conscience too;
So, I may discover my own path;
That's all I ask of you.

Listen to me Mother; listen to me Father;
With your light and wisdom; guide me on my way;
Give my your strength Mother; give me your strength Father;
So that I can learn from my own mistakes.
Maybe then, I will be able to form a point of view.
So please; encourage me; and love me;
That's all I ask of you.

Daniella J Philbin

I am Just an In-between

I am not allowed to use *make-up*!
My Father is adamant, and firm -
Other girls of my age, visit cinemas each week,
And wear nail varnish, and have their hair permed!

One girl I know - has a young man;
They take walks on the hills and beach,
I *miss out* - on all of these things. . .
Simple pleasures - but so out of reach!

I know I'm naive - and so terribly shy;
'You're too young!' - my Father will say -
'For meetings, or outings, or strolls with boys -
Rome wasn't built in a day!'

My apparel is juvenile, *work-a-day plain*,
My hair is straight - short with a fringe -
I'm not *one of the crowd* who share new freedoms -
They tease me - and their taunts make me cringe!

My cousins are visiting from Canada;
Both about the same age as me -
They wear *Teddy Bear* coats and sheer silken hose -
High-heeled court shoes, and fine jewellery!

Their underwear really makes me *drool*;
Crepe-de-chine panties and slips:
Whilst I still wear *lib-bodice* and petticoat,
Directaire knickers and *granny-like stockings* - thick!

I'm hoping things will improve quite soon -
When in January, I will reach sixteen; -
And leave *that era* behind, of *being seen, and not heard!*
And the agonising nondescript of this *in-between!*
Gertrude Parsons

From a Train

Tall poplars, grey and gaunt
Against the snowy landscape;
A long muddy lane, low-hedged
Beneath me as I look out.

One boy walks the lane, schoolbag
Slung over his shoulder, meandering
Like a slow sluggish river, reluctant
To meet the roar of the sea.

And Shakespeare lives again.

Richard Stewart

Take Things Easy

Dear friends, I'm sure
You will all agree,
There's almost nothing
Worse to see
Than powers of thinking
Rust and freeze
And a brain becoming
As soft as cheese.
Take things easy
Take your time
Don't let school
Clog and clutter your mind.

There's no earthly
Way of knowing
In which direction
We are going.
Caught in the struggle
Of another day
You may long for shores
So far away.
Send a postcard to
Remind yourself
That school could never
Seriously affect your health.

So, take things easy,
As I've told you,
And do your best,
That's all you can do.

Patrick Hennessy

Her Dream is Her Own

She believed herself to be a star
Yet at every audition she was told to
Try again next time
She thought she had performed brilliantly,
Only her Mother agreed.
Underneath her zealous façade,
She was still a young teenager
With a delicate heart
That could easily be broken
And which happened after every audition
She knew she would never
Make it on Broadway,
But still, she dreamt,
Believing her dreams were sacred, personal and private
As they were her own aspirations.
Little did she know,
That in this world
Even dreams can be invaded.

Lisa M Thomas

Teenage Blues

Mum and Dad can be such a pain,
They keep moaning because I'm late home again,
Sister Kate can do no wrong,
It makes me sick all day long.

My mates all came around last night,
I thought I would give them all a bite,
This morning Mum's in such a mood,
She said we had nicked all the food.

Sister Sue is in love again,
Moping all around she's such a pain,
If only she would understand,
It's such a folly to trust any man.

We have got to sit A levels soon,
If we pass it will be a boom,
Swotting up all day long,
Have I got it right or is it wrong.

University is our goal,
Got no time to Rock and Roll,
Hope our Degrees will have some worth,
Before grown ups destroy the Earth.

I'll borrow some money for new gear,
I've got to give myself some cheer,
Mum and Dad are not too bad,
They say I'm just a Jack the Lad.

When I finally leave my teens,
Someone else can have my jeans,
Don't laugh too much if I seem glum,
For you may have your time to come.
Jim Wilson

Crisis Incognito

It seemed, for the boy, to be far greater
To live for today, and to grow up later.
It seemed, for the girl, the thing to be done:
To meet with a boy, and experience *fun*.

After class - it was ever so tedious French -
The girl met with the boy on a playing-field bench.
A kiss - not French, but really quite sweet -
Preceded the way for a sexual treat.

Later that night, on the same bench once more,
The girl, with the boy, and her thoughts of before, said,
'Sex is the name of the game for tonight.'
The boy was prepared for erotic delight.

The girl then did stop when nothing was done
For protection against the results of such *fun*.
The boy was annoyed when the girl so declined:
But, with AIDS, thought the girl, *if we died, who would mind?*

Nathaniel Conway

First Heart's Abduction

I have been abducted,
abducted by an arrow,
an arrow from her heart to mine.
I tried to struggle,
deny her and escape.
I know she is harmless,
yet I am harmful.
She has sent me a message -
a curt note in childish letters,
I am to meet her, alone.
I am trapped,
trapped by this arrow,
I feel claustrophobic,
there has to be a mistake,
she can't mean me -
I don't even know what love is!
I'm terrified, unsure and uncertain -
what do I do,
I've been cruelly taken,
taken by abduction,
an abduction from the heart.

D A Lowe

I'd Rather be a Tomboy

Pretty girl with a pout
Pretty girl with a dimple
Pretty girl who shouted out
Why can't I be plain and simple
All the boys are after me
They pester me night and day
I'm not full of fun and fancy free
With me they won't have their wicked way
A boy should be just a friend
To talk of love is daft, I said
And spotty Gavin was just the end
I told him promptly, drop dead.

Robin Barker

A Kiss

A kiss can be so delightful
Can make you very excitable.
It can be wet! Like a fish
You can even kiss a dish.
Thin lip kisses are so grim
Sort of catch you on the chin.
Dribbly ones are horrid
Can make you rather worried.
If someone has the flu!
What should you do?
Always be sure to check
Then give them just a peck.

Nancy Eleanor Smith

For Kay, my First Love

You were only fourteen, in the flower of your youth.
I was two years older, but much slower.
I never said I loved you, although that was the truth.
I'd never been out with a girl before.

You taught me how to kiss you. It was really my first time,
And though that kiss was fairly brief and fleeting,
Quite suddenly, to my surprise, you touched your tongue on mine,
And I could taste the sweet that you'd been eating.

You took me to your garden shed, and if we should be caught,
I was to say you're showing me your rabbit,
And when you leaned against me, in a way that made me hot,
I didn't know that this was just your habit.

Maybe I was stupid, but I had such respect.
I tried to keep my basic instincts hidden,
But later, when I heard you'd slept with other boys, I checked,
And found that I'm the *only* one you didn't!

Lawrence Stewart

Bike Sheds

Let's go behind the bike sheds
and smoke a little pot
the teachers will never see us
we haven't got a lot.

A quick few puffs and we're away
upon a lovely cloud
keep Sarah quiet or they'll hear
she's laughing now out loud.

I know I'm only very young
but there is no need to fret
I can give it up tomorrow
do you want to bet?

I often take some tablets
as well as smoking pot
I won't get hooked like others
as I do not take a lot.

I've been offered lots of drugs
at school and home as well
teenagers in this world today
think it is really swell.

I've lost lots of weight and I am spotty
they say it's through the drugs
and that people who smoke pot
are just a load of mugs.

PS They're right!

Tracie Austin

Privacy?

You would think that by now
That I would be understood
But progress hasn't even taken place
(If there is a place)

All those years of trying
Hasn't even made them flinch
They still haven't got a clue
That privacy means so much to me

All I ever wanted, was to have my own privacy
A room with a door, and nobody could come in and pester me
It's a simple wish, but it's all I wanted
Privacy means a lot to me.

They thought that my life was all a big game
But to this day, my name is still at the bottom of the list
Would you believe that TV is to blame
(I think you should)

To even try and make them understand
Would be like trying to make a stone bleed
Their poor attitudes make me realise
That the only thing that matters
Is for me to have strong beliefs

I don't know how they can possibly carry on
When their track records are hardly clean
To them my name could be Hilary or John
They don't even know that I am here

It was all that I ever wanted, to have my own privacy
A room with a door, and nobody could come in and pester me
It's a simple wish, but it's all I wanted
Privacy means a lot to me.

Tony Watson

Youth

My child you are but young today,
And may resent us in a way
When we give advice we think is right
That is the time you start to fight.
Your blood's afire you act hastily
Then wonder why these things should be
When everything does not go your way,
You tend to forget there's another day.
You start to learn by your mistakes
If you have got what it takes;
So don't resent an elder's view
Remember we were young once, just like you.
We learned the hard way of life's rule
And this came after we'd left school.
The path of life is sometimes stoney
And you'll learn to judge the real from the *phoney*.
Everything is not always as it seems
And sometimes we have broken dreams,
But as you grow older and realise
You'll grow far better and more wise
If you will listen now and then, you won't be disillusioned when
Your dreams fall through, you'll start again
To build your hopes on a good, firm foundation,
With hard work and plenty of determination
For nothing comes the easy way
For everything in life you must pay
Whether it be sweat or blood
You'll have to work for all that's good,
And when you've reached your highest peak,
You will be strong instead of weak.

Mona Pounder Bulmer

Black Leather Jacket

Ugh! What a jacket my Mother cried in disbelief
You're not wearing that or being seen out with me
Why is it when I wear my black leather jacket
People give me a uniformed identity
But on a bike it's what I need
I'd look pretty silly in an evening gown and a string of pearl beads
I love my bike and I love my Mother
But I also love my jacket
Even though it makes me look tougher

Cate Arculeo

Growing Pains

Getting to thirteen,
Feeling the change
Parents watching, sighing,
Question? Are you alright,

Don't forget in at eight,
Homework to be done
Have you a boyfriend,
All in the one breath,

Seventeen, a lovely age,
Pimples, and fat gone
Able to stay out
Without a shout,

Courting, a game of chance,
Who knows, if it's Mr Right,
They tell me, you will know.
Now at nineteen, I'll hope.

Florence Roberts

I Leave Tomorrow

I leave tomorrow. Can I let the train move me out
Lean back in a corner seat, leave without a shout?
No camera cocked its eye and impressed your image
But you are in my mind and not a dreamer's image.
My throat thirsts. I have no camel's hump to loot.
My heart is hollow, such hurting, but I must afoot.
At least we met. That pain of parting I must manage
In clutching the cameo of your coming as the salvage.

I leave tomorrow . . .

Valley March

Break

The reverent joy of a girl and a boy in love.
Laughter and light for a life to be lived as one.
A stone falls to the bottom of a waterless well.

Audrey Gorle

The Leaving

Early to bed and early to rise
Breakfast on the table
What would you say upon leaving home
To please myself not listen to
To face a world so different now
From what it was when I was born

How to tell them I wish to leave
To leave the fold where I was born
You looked after me all this time
A shelter from the wind and rain
This home so many years have flown
Now I wonder to start alone

It's not the leaving that hurts me so
But watching you as I leave to go
So many times when troubles grew
You were always there no matter what
For I can leave this place this home
To go out in the world alone

Don't tell me now you would miss me so
To make me stay and change my mind
So open the door and let me go
You standing there in front of me
Those eyes that looked your way so long
Shall find a place in life as strong

Now to please myself when I arise
This time I chose to lay my head
To fetch my breakfast and clean up too
For only myself to care for now
But to think it was so hard at home
One should try living on one's own
W J Orange

Don't Want to Know

When a friend of a friend,
Tells you they don't want to know
How your friend is feeling,
That they're feeling low.
Talk awhile to them
Help them to understand:
Your friend needs their support,
With your help, they can!

When the mother of your friend,
Doesn't want to talk to you;
They've heard the rumours and the gossip,
And don't want them to be true!
Then you know you are on your own;
Visit your friend who's depressed and alone.
Take their hand and hold it tight
Lead them through their *marish-night*.
When they find they're at the end
They'll call to you, their true friend!

Deborah Collins

My Teenage Daughter

Mum, can I borrow your coat,
Mum, will you fix my hair,
Mum, I'll be late for the bus,
Mum, don't you care!
Mum, help me with my homework,
Mum, keep my sister quiet.
Mum, there's this boy I fancy,
Mum, the disco is tonight,
Mum, can I go to the pictures,
Mum, can I please, please.
Mum, I'll help you do the dishes,
Mum, in a minute, I'll just do this.
Mum, Take That are on TV.
Mum, look Jason Donovan too.
Mum, will you buy me a T-shirt,
Mum, I've got nothing to wear.
Mum, Mum, where are you,
Mum, will you take me to the bus,
Mum, thanks for the new dress,
Mum, I really do love you.

Hazel Jackson

Spots

You can pop them, squash them,
Splat them and wash them -
But they'll never go away!
You can use the creams, the gels, the soaps -
Every single day!

You can take up make-up,
To hide the facial break up -
But that just makes them worse!
You can shout and bawl, and thump the wall -
You can yell, and scream and curse!

But there is a cure,
But be rid of them for sure,
So try it - don't be a dope!
Scrub your face, night and day -
With ordinary water and soap!

Elizabeth Swanson

Too Small to Fight

So long,
it's hard to believe,
I never knew anything at all.
How could I live for fifteen years
and never know a thing.

I can't really know myself,
what a fool I've been,
it's so easy to believe
you know everything,
when you know nothing.

Too small to fight,
I was content
to conjure up words
from broken down dreams,
with the looks I wore
how could I concede.

My world was to wander,
I lived for adventure.
Today is a festival,
life is wonderful,
that's how it should be.

David Quick

Pure Pleasure

At my school
clever people did Latin
not so clever people did Physics
not clever people did Cookery.

Amo amas amat
yawned me to sleep.

Sixth form students
made Celebration Cakes
as an optional extra.

Pounds of ingredients
elbow greased
in the days before mixers.

Hours of enjoyment
trellised icing layered with love.

I carried the cake
to my Grandparents' house
and surprised them in the hall.

'This is for your golden wedding,' I said.

My grandmother admired it profusely.

My grandfather cried.

Daphne Harrall

Teenage Revolt

Your mind wears the talisman
'Tis a symbol of youth
Planted in childhood between passion and truth
Your mask wears the battle of a social assault
Who paint abstract innuendoes of a teenage revolt

Your voice is the future
Your candle must glow
Yonder lies the answers which you already know
Your mind hides a figure your conscience can't flout
At home sits a mother still covered in talc

A war of intrusion
Not a battle they choose
Whole worlds fall apart when the parents intrude
Come each generation the quarrel is one
Between mother and daughter and father and son

The pendulum swaggers
Amid moments of truce
Between bouts of depression the armies produce
Your eyes see a jungle 'tween steeples of hope
Built on words leading nowhere which Society wrote

They're not the authors
But the victims of birth
Just Society pilgrims searching the temples of earth
The march beyond childhood 'tis nobodies fault
Following God's secret pilgrimage through the teenage revolt

David Bridgewater

The Love I Lost Long Ago

It's getting late,
And I listen to that old record.
Atmospheres surrounding me,
Reminding me,
The love I lost long ago.

So the song said it all,
Love her before I knew her name.
And I still feel a chill when I remember her face, her touch.

However brief our encounter,
My memory recalls that Summer's day like it was yesterday.
Light-hearted laughter mixed with heartache and pain,
And remembering how close I was, in the rain, that Summer's night.
So very close,
So very close.

It's getting late,
The old record dies,
And I realise,

I will never change the past.

But I'll never forget,
I'll never forget.

The love I lost long ago.

Darren Powell

Over the Threshold

If you know you really have
Done your very best,
Put away your homework books,
And lay you down to rest,
Tomorrow is another day,
And as you are growing older,
You'll realise all is not lost,
Life is just a folder
Filled with many happenings,
Gathered through the years,
Times of wonderful happiness,
And heartbreaking tears.
So put your best foot forward,
Clench your fists and lift your chin,
Onward, forever onward,
To bring the rich harvest safely in.

Frances Hickman-Robinson

The Love and Understanding of a Teenager

I've been through a lot these past few years
There's been some laughter, but mostly tears
First of all there was meeting you
My parents telling me what to do
'You can't wear that,' my Mum would say
Dad would look, then turn away
Why can't anyone understand me?
Just open your eyes, and you might see
I'm just a teenager and that is all
Why did you make me feel so small?
I thought you loved me, I thought you cared
My thoughts with you are what I shared
But on top of this I went to school
I never obeyed every rule
And then there's that time, when you get your first spot
And trying creams, that don't work a lot
You went off with my best friend
You said our love would never end
You didn't tell me, you didn't say
You just went and ran away
How could you leave me all alone
You didn't even care to phone
When you went you made Mum and Dad glad
They didn't care that I was sad
You said you loved me or was that maybe
But don't you know I'm carrying your baby?
Why can't anyone understand me?
Just open your eyes and you might see
I'm just a teenager and that is all
Why did you make me feel so small?. . .

Kelly Swinscow (15)

Speaking Without Listening

'It's the real thing, you can't beat the feeling,
Our fizzy pop drinks will send your mind reeling.
It will be *you* the pretty girls will come round to see.'
'Look at the dove flying so high,' said he.

'Now listen to me carefully you willing young man
Buy now, pay later is my interest-free plan.
Our financial wizards will make you money.'
'Oh didn't you know I'm in love,' said he.

'Ultra, super-concentrated is the solution
To save you young kids from adult disillusion.
Your whiter than white lives must have security.'
'All we want is to be happy,' said he.

Jeff Day

Spider Girl

Teetering on tiptoe
(steps echoing
stiletto heels)
there she goes -
the skinny-jeaned
black widow
of a thousand streets

to wait white-faced
beneath a neon flare,
with tarry hair
pomaded into spikes.

Beside graffiti web
this latter-day Arachne dreams -

does she search puddles
for reflections
of a former self

hoping perhaps
that next year's image
will be wreathed
in daisy chains. . .

Josie Davies

Uncertainty

Change alter, up and down
Begin then end again
Nothing's ever constant
Nothing stays the same
Find a happy place
Then something interferes
Disrupts, turns you upside down
Resurfacing your fears
When you find your balance
Someone pushes you
Getting used to something
Then forced to something new
Back forward, up and down
Right way and inside out
Always moving, changing
Every moment one of doubt

Claire Dannatt

The Homeless Teenager

I had no choice but to roam.
I could not stand the noise at home;
The rows between my Mum and Dad
With fights and swearing got so bad:
It almost drove me mad!

DHSS rules forbid
Handouts to a homeless kid
Underage, and no one cares
To interfere with kids' affairs.
All people do is stare.

I'm filled with dread; the rats abound
In this old barn; their gnawing sound
Goes on all night. Fear makes me weep.
I feel so cold, I can not sleep.
My spirit is sunken deep.

Dear Guardian Angel, guide me right
Into a future where I might
Be able to stand on my own two feet,
And have enough stamina to beat
The hurdles I may meet.

Many years have passed me by
Since I begged for you to try
To guide me from the life I had
When I'd left my Mum and Dad.
You help when times were bad.

The fruitful years I've had since then
Have stabilised me once again.
I have a home where love thrives in it.
But I do *not* forget - not for one minute,
What I've been through - to win it.

Tina Macinnes

Henry

Henry was a freckled, fourteen year old lad.
Henry went to church on Sundays with his Mum and Dad.

Henry met me when I was twelve and gave me my first kiss.
Henry caught me by surprise, he grabbed, aimed and missed!

Henry was cross, 'You're supposed to close your eyes,' he cried.
Henry kissed me again, I peeped a little, 'That's better,' he sighed.

Henry smiled and tapped my nose, mounted his bike and rode into the square.
Henry sadly went crashing to the ground when Mum yelled, 'Oi you down there!'

Henry sped away not knowing that Mum was joking, tears of laughter on her face.
Henry? I never saw him again not even at church, he disappeared without a trace.

C P Hall

Spotty Me

I was feeling very sprightly
When I got up today.
The sun was shining brightly
And my friend had come to say.

Until that was, I looked and saw
A great big purple spot.
I know it wasn't there before,
It really felt quite hot.

A great big blob that seemed to glow,
You could not fail to see.
The more I looked, it seemed to grow.
It seemed so big to me.

Stuck right there upon my cheek,
For everyone to see,
It wasn't there this time last week.
I wish I wasn't me.

Gillian M Thomson

Growing Pains

It's long ago now but looking back, I remember my teenage years
What sort of life was in store, no one knew the sorrows and tears.
I hated being in service, that life was not for me
While cleaning the coals next morning dreaming, how nice to be free,
I slipped off my apron, put on my coat, then ran as fast as I dare
My destination was homeward bound, I arrived without a care.

Two days later my Mother said, 'I must have money for your keep.'
I found myself work at a printers, and thought this will do me a treat.
I settled in nicely and did my job well, staying there for six years
Every one friendly and helpful, no worries and no fears.
I made plenty of friends, boy's short and tall
We met Saturday nights at the old village hall.

Good times we had, but boys were a pain
Football and swimming all out in the rain.
Those teenage years were not all that bad
Not like today, where for some life's so sad.
What can we do to help them find employment
Love them and pray that God gives them patience.

Lilian Ware

What is a Teenager?

A teenager, I think you'll find,
Is one who's nearly left behind,
Their carefree youth and carefree mind,
A child and adult both combined.

A difficult time, with changes and fears,
Of an unknown life in later years,
Their heads are full of strange ideas,
And confrontations end in tears.

A parent has to be their guide,
Stand up for them and take their side,
Shelter them on life's roller-coaster ride,
And dispel insecurities that they hide.

There'll be many a night Mum and Dad will wait,
When their *little girl* will stay out late,
She then returns in a drunken state,
Under the influence of her best mate.

It doesn't matter what the adults say,
They'll always go their own sweet way,
One can only hope that they will stay
On the road to success, and not be led astray.

Valerie Woodward

Careers

We've been summoned by the Headmaster
it's school leaving day today
he's going to give us his blessing
sending us on our way.
The subject of careers came up first
what are you doing Ted?
I'm going to work in a bank
what are you doing Fred?
I'm being a motor mechanic
servicing buses that go on the road.
A fashion model was Sue's vocation
wearing clothes made A-la-mode.
Joy's going to be a secretary
Bill's training to be a vet
where are you going to work Mary?
We haven't heard you yet.
I had been keeping my mouth shut
trying to stay out of sight
I hadn't done very well at school
except in English and art.
Come along Mary please don't be shy
said the Headmaster peeling a cox's
how embarrassing what could I say
I'm going to put labels on boxes.

Marjorie Mary Pearson

Romance

He had a wood leg
And a glass eye
that turned.
And a look on his face
Like a man who'd
been spurned.

He never once smiled
Well he couldn't
alas.
For his false teeth were placed
on a shelf
in a glass.

Jug handles for ears
And a deep chin
(or two)
No wonder she left him
You'd not want him
would you?

Standing out in the crowd
He was tall for
his age.
Wearing green spotted socks
Well he looked all
the rage.

Then to his delight
And his heart filled
with glee.
He met a young lady.
She was just four
foot three!

Now they can both be found
Hand in hand by
the shore.
She looks into his eyes
(If he kneels on
the floor!)

As the moonlight beams down
And reflects on
his socks.
She reached up for a kiss
('Cos she carries
a box!)

Kate McNamara

The Breeze is Silent (a Study of Virginity)

The breeze is silent
in my unusual forest.
Since its conception the breeze
has regarded my starched leaves as
a private larynx.

Now the coppice is unyielding
the aerial torrents blow undetected.
The precision of communication is surely lost
and I only recognise a buffeting conversation.

Despite the tender nature of my fibre,
a physical colloquy
is less passionate than the familiar soliloquy.
If the leaves re-bud,
and the breeze speaks again,
I will receive you.

Alex Smith

Crazy Mixed Up Kid

You said you'd come at half past one, but yes you're always late.
I'm looking out the window. You're walking past our gate.
Who's that dishy blonde you're with? Some long lost cousin I'll bet.
The same old story all the time. Don't worry, I'll get you yet.

Last week you said, 'I'm working late,' but I know where you went.
Down to the pub to have a drink. And then those flowers you sent!
Were they to show undying love to me and your one and only?
Or were they just to make me feel a little bit less lonely.

I know your tricks. I see you games. I hear your lies each night.
But if you think I'll wait around, then you're in for a fright.
For Dave should be in half an hour. He's quiet, not like you.
I think I'll leave my dreams behind, and start my life anew.

But wait, you're coming back again. You're walking up our path.
And where's the girl that you were with whose looks I'd like not half.
Oh here we go, that same old tale, your long lost cousin from Spain.
You look so cute just standing there, your face wet from the rain.
Did I just say I didn't want to see you again?
On second thoughts, I've changed my mind. Welcome home darling.

Ruth Mackrell

First Date

A date with that boy,
Oh, what a joy.

What shall I wear?
In green I look like a pear.

I'm so fat in red,
I wish I was dead.

I'm so thin in brown,
I look like a clown.

I'm not bad in blue,
So that will have to do.

What about my hair,
Oh help, I despair.

Now my face,
What an awful disgrace.

I looked a perfect rose,
Until I saw a pimple on my nose.

Then a spot on my chin,
I just can't win.

I can't go, I said,
And hid my head.

'It's you, he asked out,'
Cried Mum, with a shout.

Not your nose, or your hair,
So do you think he will care.

Mum was right,
We had a wonderful night.

Maureen B Fitzgerald

Girls Honour Your Bodies

Girls, *honour* your bodies
Because they are often *misused*
Girls, *honour* your bodies
Because some *men* often *abuse*
The closeness of lovemaking
To *many* it's just sex
And as soon as they've finished with you
They're on to the *next*!

Girls, *honour* your bodies
Like a temple of gold
And any wishing they're not virgins
It's a special privilege to hold.
It's *too* easy to do it
With many a man
But far harder to hold out
So wait if you can!
So wait until you know
And you feel that he's right.
Not after a few drinks
At a party one night!
Because regretting your actions
Is the most painful of all
And feeling *used and abused*
Because he just didn't *call*!

Ayesha Shelley Adonais

The Teenage Years

The teenage years
are full of woes
lots of tears
Mum's raving Dad's real mad
could I be this bad
the teenage years
with fights and brawls
no one knows what pressure
reigns
for a teenager it's such
a strain
oh what a pain
here it comes again.

Margaret Hickman

Growing Pains

There is a subtle change in our household
which at times causes rather a strain
brought to the surface by someone
and laughingly called growing pains!
That someone is my lovely daughter
when little - was dainty and sweet
but please can other Mums tell me
why they wear great boots on their feet.
The staying out late is a challenge
I'm sure we weren't that bad
if the choice comes in asking permission
she would rather deal with her Dad.
The cares of the world rest with her
she shoulders them best as she can
'til the changing mood gives a swing upwards
making another part of life's plan.
I know it's not easy for youngsters
and I sympathise - really I do
but please could you vacate the bathroom
I'm really in need of the loo.
Now here comes the cry we all wait for
the one which drives Mums to despair
I'm in desperate need of some new clothes
for I haven't a damn thing to wear!

Hilary Malone

Fourteen

My memories I'll not forget,
Of my teenage years you can bet,
I'll remember all the things then,
Like when I became aware of men!
Must have been around fourteen,
When my spot's were the only important thing,
Puppy fat everywhere,
Why do I have such greasy hair?
Who do I have to come home early?
I'm old enough to stay out surely,
My friend next door stays out till late,
And I can't be a second late!
Or my life would suffer,
No freedom for a week,
I decided a better life I'd seek,
I'll go away leave home tonight,
I'll go so quietly so not to fight,
I know the pavements are gold out there,
Do what I want,
No one to care.

But it's not so good after all,
Freezing cold pavements,
Buildings too tall,
I'll go home now,
To my nagging mum,
And say I'm sorry that the time has come,
To grow up now to be more bold,
To do whatever I am told!

R Barlow

Give it a Rest Mum

Don't worry Mum, I won't be late.
Yes that's right, I'm off on a date.
Of course it's with a girl.
And yes she's nice, dark-haired and pretty.
How old - I haven't asked her yet,
About fifteen I guess, her name by the way is Annette.

Thanks Mum, but I'm OK for money.
It's a special film we're seeing, supposed to be funny.
No I won't do anything silly. What do you mean
Behave ourselves in the back row.
Is that where you and Dad sat all those years ago.
Come off it Mum, I'm sixteen years old,
Not a little boy anymore for you to scold.

Yes Mum, I have changed my socks.
I wish you'd stop worrying, you do carry on.
I'll be home by eleven I promise.
No I don't need a lift, I'm taking the bus,
For God's sake mum don't make such a fuss.
I know you mean well, you do what you think is best.
But please Mum old darling, just give it a rest.

David Wicking

My Teens

Now that I am in My Teens,
I wear Baggy Shirts and Scruffy Jeans,
Trainer Shoes, Grown-Up Socks,
Do not always Comb my Locks,
Ride a Bike, Kick a Football around,
Pocket Money's gone up a Pound,
I play up Mum, and play up Dad,
Sometimes I'm really Very Bad,
But Mum knows that I love her,
No matter what I do,
It's just that Growing Up these days,
Seems Very Hard to do.

P A Burton-Westcott

The Day of Judgement

Another five minutes, then I'll try to forget
and pretend today hasn't come.
All senses alert for the usual steps, which
yesterday were merely routine.
Panic invades as a voice in my head tells me
surely that's someone outside.
But reason prevails as I sit down again
and count off another five minutes.

A sharp click from downstairs,
then soft thud on the mat,
brings dread right into my heart.
Faltering steps to the head of the stairs
and there - down below - is the *word.*

The noise in my head from my poor pounding heart
is made worse by my fumbling fingers,
as they wrestle with paper that won't come unstuck
and let the contents be free.
Seconds pass like hours, a lifetime at stake,
my prayer streams out like a flood
'Dear God - help me now, just for once let it say
two wonderful *A's* and a *B*.'

Irene Campbell

Only Seventeen

Who desecrated the rainforests for the sake of some posh wood
Wasn't me I'm only seventeen I'd stop them if I could
Who slaughters gentle cows and lambs and who feels no remorse
Not me I'm only seventeen I know it's wrong of course

Who is it pollutes the sea killing whales and fish
Never me I'd like to save them all but I can only wish
Who civilizes lost tribes till they slowly disappear
Don't want them gone forever seventeen cries a silent tear
And who is it that wants this world wantonly shattered apart
Ain't me I'm only seventeen and it's sadly breaking my heart

I'd recreate the forests now
And set the pig the sheep and cow
Free to wander the earth in good faith

I'd ban ships on the ocean
What dolphins in motion
And make sure foxes were safe

I'd stop all wars and atrocity
Life would know no animosity
All creatures free from misery
Cos this world means a lot to me

Yeah I can put this earth right well I can have my dream
I'm just about to walk life's road I'm only seventeen.

Emile Ewe

Unwilling Witness

The rain is falling on my head,
The wind is blowing hard,
And I wish that I had stayed in bed.
Is it any different where you are?

Oh I think that I will go insane!
There are voices screaming in my soul;
I see you living life so well.
Do you never feel the cold?

Why do I see the things I do?
A world of ruin and decay!
Surely I am not the only one to see;
How I wish that it would go away!

People wander down the tunnels that they made,
Ever tireless on their narrow way;
Like clockwork zombies on parade
They try to keep reality at bay.

Is this something only I can feel?
Something only I can know?
I drive my head against a wall;
There is nowhere left for me to go.

So here I stand alone,
Unwilling witness to the turning wheel of time.
I watch as each new thunderbolt is thrown;
Soon you will pay for your passive crime.

Philip J Faulkner

Teenage Tears

Thank goodness I'm no longer young -
I couldn't stand the strain,
It's bad enough remembering
The problems and the pain.

Now, falling in and out of love
Was all I seemed to do,
Each boyfriend was my *hearts desire*
Till I found someone new.

The make-up I would plaster on -
The clothes that I would buy,
The money that I spent on them
Now makes me want to cry!

I do recall the day I bleached
My hair - and it dropped out!
And Dad, he was so very cross -
Oh dear, how he did shout!

Those awful times when I would blush -
My face I'd try to hide,
I couldn't overcome being shy
No matter how I tried.

And oh, those dreaded pimples
And spots that drove me mad,
A smoother skin I longed to have
But somehow never had.

Yes, I am happy where I am -
Now in my middle years,
I wouldn't want to feel again
The flow of teenage tears.

Briony V Lill

That Day in May

The buttercups along the way,
Such golden gems that day in May,
We paused at times, to meet the gaze
Of Mother Sun - her glinting rays.

Beyond the field - a stream we found,
And on its bank - soft mossy ground
We sat together, hand in hand,
Just dreaming of a wonderland.

The rippling water - crystal clear,
Such charm of countryside so dear,
The echo of a bouncing stone,
And weeds around so overgrown.

Marsh - marigolds in stately pose
And celandines beneath our toes,
The bluebells peeping in the glade,
Their nodding heads - the scene surveyed.

The lively humming of the bees
And birds in flight above the trees,
Their serenade it filled the air
With mirth and laughter everywhere.

We chatted long, our eyes both met
I heard him whisper, 'You're my pet.'
And then, an interlude of bliss
With lips pressed close - a lingering kiss.

With ecstasy within my heart
I did so hope we would not part,
The lovelight gleamed on world serene,
That day in May - at seventeen.
Joan Higgins

The Idealists

You lordly ones possess the earth
But, careless of your wealth,
You seem to scorn delight and mirth
Scarce giving thanks for life or birth,
And praising, if at all, by stealth.

Do you conceal from older eyes
The joys that once were ours?
Do you experience ecstasies
Such as we learned to memorise
Against the time of failing powers?

Enjoy your riches while you may;
Drink while the cup is filled.
Dragons will still be here to slay,
Truth will wait for another day
And wisdom's voice will not be stilled.

Too soon the rose will lose its scent,
The robin cease to sing,
No sun will gild the firmament,
Trees will be bare, their branches bent
And ice will seal the forest spring.

Norman Stampfer

New Girl in School

She walked slowly to the classroom
Having nerves feelings of doom
She peeked her head round the door
She stuck like glue to the floor

The door opened and there she stood
She hid her face with her hood
Everybody began to stare
At the girl with long red hair

The teacher bellowed, *come here!*
Come on my dear,
There she stood with freckled face
Wishing she hadn't come to this place.

Kelly Anne Costley

Growing Pains

There was a handsome boy at school
He was the girl's delight
I would hide when he came in sight
Sport day came, there he was
In white shorts, those legs, so strong and tan.

He smiled and said 'Hello'
Asked me for a date
My friends they envied me
They never thought, he would fancy me

I met the boy named Stanley
We laughed and talked
What a happy pair we were

I was late, I ran home
My Father was not pleased, with Stanley
For keeping me out late
So that was the end of Stanley
And my first date.

Mary Hobday

Teenage Dilemma

I vigorously wipe the mirror,
Though I know that it's in vain,
The three red spots upon my chin,
Mockingly remain.
How can I go to school like this?
Disfigured? My life is a sham,
My thighs are fat, I hate my hair
Now Zits! I'm cursed. I am.
Why was I born so ugly?
It really isn't fair,
No other girls of my age
Have the problems I must bear.
Still my Dad says that I'm beautiful
And boys still ask me out,
So I can't be that bad can I?
'Where's your make-up Mum,' I shout!

T J Griffin

Menstruation Lamentation

In case I'm dead tomorrow,
I am leaving them this note.
In the midst of all their sorrow
They can say, at least, She Wrote.

It began when Amy said,
'I Became A Woman Today,'
It just went through my head
To say I had started yesterday.

I didn't mean to lie
But I needed to save face.
It was either that, or cry,
She would have done the same in my place.

She could have taken it much better
If I'd been excused from showers.
Because Mum wouldn't write a letter
I had to lie to her for hours.

Discussions, long and tedious,
Between us daily grow
And all to do with periods,
About which, I still don't know!

Mum says I could go ages yet
She sometimes drives me wild.
She won't smile as much, I bet,
When there is no darling Grandchild.

Well, I was going to commit Suicide.
Quietly. Calm and formal.
But now, I can put Death aside,
It appears I'm perfectly normal.
Cheryl Howarth

The Misunderstanding

Why did I act that way?
Those harsh words uttered.
If only time I could stay,
to unravel the chain of circumstance.

I wanted so to be loved by all,
be clever, witty and pretty,
grown up, graceful and tall.
Oh, why could no-one understand me?

You said, I changed over night,
a little girl, no more.
Sweetness, innocence, a smile so bright,
now cynical and out of reach.

Underneath the bright made-up face,
high-heels, tight skirts and carefree manner;
my heart remained in a tight-locked case,
bewildered, frightened and misunderstood.

All I needed was a little time,
to progress naturally,
My heart cried out, *I've done no crime.*
I'm just completely *misunderstood.*

S B Lunnon

School Swot

Imprisoned
On a pedestal
Of other peoples'
Praise

All eyes on me
Waiting for me to fall
So they can laugh.

I see you
At the back of the crowd
My single friend

Your eyes tell me
Something different
That you would rescue me
But cannot bear
To take on
The hatred of your crowd.
You are not strong enough.

I want to say
It doesn't matter
But it does

I want to say
The crumbs of your friendship
Are enough.

Christine Lang

Unemployed

They wake
to diaries' blank page

and no one calls:
'Time you were off!'

In a roomful of gloom
they say: 'I don't care.'

They wake
but wish they hadn't

and don't jump out of bed.
The weight of the day

anchors them there
in despair.

The poet: 'Seize hope in your pain
                  and try: trying again.'

Anne Shells

First Love False Love

Here I'm sitting all alone
Waiting for my love to phone,
Waiting by a phone which never rings.
Outside my window a blackbird sings
And Spring bursts forth in glorious green.
Deserted I watch this gorgeous scene
And yet my heart is full of misery,
Untouched by Nature's gown of beauty.
Summer clad in emerald hue,
Arrives but still no word from you
To stir my heart so full of sadness;
So out of step with Nature's gladness.
Still I wait when Autumn's browns
Paint the leaves which tumble down,
With brown and yellow, red and gold,
As another year grows tired and old,
And soon instead of Autumn leaves
The silent snow falls, still I grieve,
For still alone, I hope, I wait,
My silent loving turns to hate,
And as I survey Winter's icy blue,
My heart too, is cold when I remember you.
Spring returns and still alone,
I mourn a love who's upped and flown;
Not even March can shed a tear,
As sad as I in contemplation of a lonely year,
And tears I'll shed, till my heart bursts
For teenage first love hurts the worst.

Sarah Hartwell

Full Circle

I used to be a teenager, several years ago -
I was a 60's baby, brought up with Manilow.
We were the same, we all had spots, (but we used Clearasil).
We weren't all green and friendly, and no-one talked about The Pill.

Wedge shoes, ponchos, jellybeans, they were all the mode,
Now it's designer labels and rucksacks for the road.
There was Spandau and Depeche Mode, Adam Ant and Fame,
Though Nation-Wide did not survive, Grange Hill and Generation Game.

Have made it to the 90's, but so much has changed,
These ozone-friendly teenagers seem to have rearranged,
The art of *Young and Trendy*, they are confident and cool,
It's a shock to know that most of them are still attending school.

They talk of Sonic Hedgehog, Guns and Roses and Take That,
Their language is so different, I wonder where it's at.
But they still have lots of homework, that's something I don't miss,
They still discuss their crushes, and the thought of that first kiss.

I'm glad I'm not a teenager, to go through that again!
In some things we've come full-circle, those wedge shoes are a pain!

Sharon Forsdyke

The In-Between Years

What advice can I give you teenager
To help through the in-between years?
Joys and heartaches are sure to occur,
With elation, romances and tears.

Standards are there for your learning,
Choose all your friendships with care,
It's too easy to take the wrong turning
To crime, or abuse and despair.

Always be honest and thoughtful,
Enjoy every day through and through,
Though problems will face you teenager
The reward of youth is for you.

Joyce Barker

Teardrops

Falling teardrop
Hide my pain
Change your saltwater
Into rain.
Shadow anger
hate my envy,
Save some hope
For I love thee.
Falling teardrops
From my eyes
Collect in streams
Under the skies
Shadow lust
Free from love,
Reach up high
To stars above.
Falling teardrops
From my heart
There's pain inside,
We are apart.

Donna Buckett

Mine Was a Quiet Rebellion

Mine was a quiet rebellion;
I didn't scream and shout, but spoke,
and when provoked, I bit my lip.
The chain once slipped, I didn't stay out
all night, until they both went wild;
a model child, no question.

Secrecy was essential;
sneaking in books considered out
and laying doubt in my parents' minds
that their *guidelines*, not based on trust,
unclear, unjust, deserved black looks;
such leniency potential!

This was my teenage ritual;
it gained near-freedom, opened the cage
for no more than a modest ransom.
Now, years on - although I've rights,
the bird has flown, the need is gone -
the fight has grown habitual.

Liz Hedgecock

Teenage Years

Teenage years bring hopes and fears,
As adults, we become.
Dating, fashion fancy clothes,
And having lots of fun.

Having parties every week,
Meeting all our friends.
Dancing, singing, records play,
The nights they never end.

Anxious to attract and please,
With make-up and with charm.
Hoping for a mate to court
Someone kind and warm.

We must cherish these years,
Enjoy them, whilst we can,
For soon they will be over,
Those teenage years of fun.

Ruby Anderson

Memories

I'll never forget the excitement of defiance
Smoking behind the bike shed
Skiving double maths
Boozing in the lunch hour

I'll never forget the anger of detention
The boredom of classes
The hatred for teachers and the fear of the cane

I'll never forget the smell of school dinners
Lumpy custard
Fish cakes and mushy peas

I'll never forget the undone homework
Whispering during exams
And the *could try harder* school report

I'll never forget the chewing gum under desk tops
Graffiti on toilet doors
And the condom on Miss Smith's car aerial!

I'll never forget putting glue on teacher's chair
The laughter that followed
Then being pulled by the ear

I'll never forget how quick the good-byes
Despite all we'd shared
Throughout our lives.

Tracey D P Johnston

My Years of Growing Up

Spots were an embarassment when I was twelve years old
But somehow I had a thick face and became rather bold
My hidden feelings were never shown
My features of my face were known
At the age of fifteen my spots disappeared
A relief at last, I just cheered
My eyes opened wide, boys were interested in me
We walked along the promenade and looked out to sea
Discos at the seaside ranged for all ages
Nightclubs obviously made slight changes
At seventeen, growing up and learning to mix
Going steady and getting fixed
At eighteen I thought I was an adult
Wise and intelligent, not at fault
I left home, independence seemed great
But money was never saved, I was in a state.
Letters through the post but one was a debt
I had a shock, what was my first step.
My parents pleaded come back home
You'll save more money than living on your own
Now when I turn back and detect
The life I had was not what I did expect.

Sarah Whitehead